# Cybertax

# IT Pro Practice Notes

**Published:**

*Practical Guide to IT Problem Management*
by Andrew Dixon
ISBN: 978-1-032-42225-1

*Managing Cybertax Risk and Results*
by George K. Tsantes and James F. Ransome
ISBN: 978-1-032-36067-6

**Forthcoming:**

*The Busy IT Manager's Guide to Data Recovery*
by Preston de Guise
ISBN: 978-1-032-45125-1

*Understanding Project Practices and Processes*
by Mel Bost
ISBN: 978-1-032-42225-1

# Cybertax

## Managing the Risks and Results

George K. Tsantes
James F. Ransome

CRC Press
Taylor & Francis Group

AN AUERBACH BOOK

First edition published 2023
by CRC Press
6000 Broken Sound Parkway NW, Suite 300, Boca Raton, FL 33487-2742
and by CRC Press
2 Park Square, Milton Park, Abingdon, Oxon, OX14 4RN

© 2023 George K. Tsantes and James F. Ransome
CRC Press is an imprint of Taylor & Francis Group, LLC

*Library of Congress Cataloging-in-Publication Data*
A catalog record has been requested for this book.

ISBN: 978-1-032-36068-3 (hbk)
ISBN: 978-1-032-36067-6 (pbk)
ISBN: 978-1-003-33010-3 (ebk)

DOI: 10.1201/9781003330103

Typeset in Sabon LT Pro
by DerryField Publishing Services

Some material in this book is taken from the following book written by one or both of the authors, with permission from Taylor & Francis Group:

*Core Software Security: Security at the Source* / ISBN: 978-1-4665-6095-6 / 2013

# Dedications

To the senior executives and boards of directors who are looking for a better way to manage cybersecurity across the organizations they lead.

— George K. Tsantes and James F. Ransome

This book is dedicated to the loving memory of Captain George Tsantes Jr. USN. George also dedicates this book to Joanna for all her patience and support.

— George K. Tsantes

# Contents

# Preface

In a perfect world we would not need cybersecurity. Technology would work without interference, there would be no malicious actors, and users would never make mistakes. Unfortunately, the opposite is true. Technology systems are open and invite malicious exploits, bad actors are multiplying in numbers and sophistication, and users constantly make errors that allow bad things to happen. CYBERPHOS views cybersecurity as a tax on the organization—cybertax—and as with other forms of taxation, the goal is to minimize and optimize this tax.

Cybertax encompasses all resources required to provide and prove cybersecurity. This includes prevention, monitoring, remediation, improvements, and proving. Proving is an underappreciated aspect of cybertax that comprises all assessments by business partners, auditors, and regulators. In effect, it's a tax on top of the cybertax. Proving drains resources from doing, further complicating the efficient and effective deployment of cybersecurity resources.

Complicating cybersecurity and further adding to your cybertax is that no organization is an island unto itself. In this connected world, your cybersecurity scope extends to the meta-enterprise—that is, your organization, its key vendors, advisors, and, in some cases, key customers. These extensions of your enterprise have access to your information, people, networks, and technology—all of which can be compromised to cause you harm.

For those of you who view good cybersecurity as a positive attribute for an organization, we agree that cybersecurity is an acceptable way to differentiate your organization from your competitors. That said, managing the efficiency and effectiveness of resources applied to cybersecurity is imperative for any organization. Viewing cybersecurity through the cybertax lens provides an effective way for non–cybersecurity experts in leadership to manage and govern cybersecurity in their organizations.

After years of managing cybersecurity risk using traditional methods and measures, we realized that the disconnect between leadership and the Chief Information Security Officer (CISO) will never be bridged using current strategies employed by companies. CYBERPHOS bridges the chasm between the two groups to ensure that cybersecurity will be managed rationally and effectively by providing a model that creates actionable cyber risk knowledge for business executives. CYBERPHOS delivers a continuously updated dashboard and key metrics to guide leadership's understanding of the organization's cybersecurity posture, its progress, and questions that engage both leadership and security experts in a common framework. Our objective was to create a short book to be used as a physical handout and digital download for potential customers of CYBERPHOS and those seeking better methods for governing cybersecurity risk.

Cybersecurity risk is a top-of-the-house issue for all organizations. This book is a must read for every current or aspiring executive seeking the best way to manage and mitigate cybersecurity risk. The book examines cybersecurity as a tax on the organization and charts the best ways leadership can be cybertax efficient. The book outlines questions and leadership techniques to gain the relevant information to manage cybersecurity threats and risk. The book will enable executives to:

- Understand cybersecurity risk from a business perspective
- Understand cybersecurity risk as a tax (cybertax)
- Understand the cybersecurity threat landscape
- Drive business-driven questions and metrics for managing cybersecurity risk
- Understand the Seven C's for managing cybersecurity risk

Executive leadership needs to manage cybersecurity risk like they manage other critical risks, such as sales, finances, resources, and competition. This book puts managing cybersecurity risk on an even plane with these other significant risks that demand leaderships' attention. This book strives to demystify cybersecurity to bridge the chasm from the top of the house to the cybersecurity function. We deliver actionable advice and metrics to measure and evaluate cybersecurity effectiveness across your organization. Governing the cybersecurity function is as important as governing finance, sales, human resources, and other key leadership responsibilities. Whether you sit in the C-suite, aspire to, or are on the board of directors, this book is for you.

# Acknowledgments

Without the confidence of CRC Press/Taylor & Francis Group and our editor, John Wyzalek, this book would not have been possible. John found a way to realize our vision. I thank him for his support and for his commitment to the project.

This book could not have been delivered without the guidance and patience of DerryField Publishing Services as we put together this manuscript. Please accept our heartfelt gratitude for the copyediting and layout—key to the delivery of any book. Thanks for working with us.

And last but not least, we each thank our coauthor, as well as the other core team members at CYBERPHOS—Kurt and Mario—who have joined us on this journey to prove that there is a more efficient way for executives and boards of directors to manage cybersecurity than what is the current status quo.

— George K. Tsantes and James F. Ransome

# About the Authors

**George K. Tsantes** is the cofounder and CEO of CYBERPHOS, a Software as a Service (SAAS) focused on improving cybersecurity risk governance. CYBERPHOS empowers leadership, boards of directors, C-suite executives, and private equity principals to provide focused and insightful cybersecurity governance and oversight.

Prior to the creation of CYBERPHOS, George was the Managing Partner at GT3 Consulting, a boutique consultancy focused on helping clients across a wide spectrum of industries understand and manage their cybersecurity risk. He helped clients deal with the emerging and ever-increasing security issues with mobile computing and cloud computing, as well as the challenges of protecting organizations, employees, and customers from the threats of an ever-connected world.

Prior to creating GT3 Consulting, George was a Principle at EY, where he led the firm's cybersecurity practice for the Financial Services Office (FSO). In this role, he advised many of EY's key clients across a wide range of cyber topics and projects to improve their ability to prevent, quickly detect, and remediate cybersecurity events. He spoke frequently to C-level executives and boards of directors, providing a business-focused assessment of the threat landscape and the leading cybersecurity practices across financial services and other critical infrastructure industries.

Prior to joining EY, George was Executive Vice President and Chief Technology Officer of Intersections, Inc., the leading provider of identity and credit management solutions for consumers and small businesses in North America. The patented Intersections authentication framework provides a platform to manage and integrate the disparate technology solutions for providing and managing good authentication.

Before joining Intersections, Inc., George was a partner at Accenture/Andersen Consulting, a global management consulting and technology services company. He was a key member of the Capital Markets Group, part of the firm's Financial Services practice and a member of Accenture's FSI Technology leadership. During his 19-year career with Accenture, he was an architect and specialized in helping clients assimilate emerging technologies, computing architectures, and development techniques.

George is a frequent speaker at corporate and industry events, including FS-ISAC, the Federal Trade Commission's Proof Positive, Security in Numbers, RSA Security Conference and The Voice Biometrics Conference. He is frquently quoted in business and technical publications, including the *Wall Street Journal*, Dark Reading, Fortune.com, Bank Technology News, and DJ Compliance Watch. George is a guest scientist at the Los Alamos National Laboratory. He is the lead inventor of U.S. Patent 7,333,635 B2, *Method and System for Confirming Personal Identity*, and U.S. Patent 8,117,648, *Secure Information Storage and Delivery*.

— George K. Tsantes

**Dr. James F. Ransome, PhD, CISSP, CISM,** is the Chief Scientist for CYBERPHOS, an early-stage cybersecurity startup.

Most recently, James was the Senior Director of Security Development Lifecycle Engineering for Intel's Product Assurance and Security (IPAS). In that capacity, he led a team of SDL engineers, architects, and product security experts to drive and implement security practices across the company. Prior to that, James was the Senior Director of Product Security and PSIRT at Intel Security (formerly McAfee). James's career includes leadership positions in the private and public sectors. He served in three chief information security officer (CISO) roles at Applied Materials, Autodesk, and Qwest Communications and four chief security officer (CSO) positions at Pilot Network Services, Exodus Communications, Exodus Communications—Cable and Wireless Company, and Cisco Collaborative Software Group. He has also served as Senior Vice President of Commercial Managed and Professional Security Services at SecureInfo, Inc., and as the Vice President of Integrated Security at CH2M Hill. Before entering the corporate world, he retired from 23 years of government service for supporting the U.S. intelligence community, federal law enforcement, and the Department of Defense.

James holds a PhD (https://nsuworks.nova.edu/gscis_etd/790/) in Information Systems, specializing in Information Security; a Master of Science Degree in Information Systems; and graduate certificates in International Business and International Affairs. He taught Applied Cryptography, Advanced Network Security, and Information Security Management as an Adjunct Professor in the Nova Southeastern University's Graduate School of Computer and Information Science (SCIS) Information Security Program. This graduate school is designated as a National Center of Academic Excellence in Information Assurance Education by the U.S. National Security Agency and the Department of Homeland Security.

James is a Certified Information Security Manager (CISM), a Certified Information Systems Security Professional (CISSP), and a Ponemon Institute Distinguished Fellow. He has authored or coauthored 16 books, 14 of which are focused on cybersecurity.

— James F. Ransome

# Chapter 1

# What Is Cybertax?

## 1.1 INTRODUCTION

In a perfect world, we would not need cybersecurity. Technology would work without interference, there would be no malicious actors, and users would never make mistakes. There would be no holes or errors in the code that powers technology, and communications between technologies would be secure.

Unfortunately, the opposite is true. Technology systems are open and invite malicious exploits, bad actors are multiplying in numbers and sophistication, and users constantly make errors that allow bad things to happen. The number of devices and apps connected to the Internet is growing exponentially. Cybersecurity is a necessary program for any organization or individual. It is a tax on the organization; we call this "cybertax."

## 1.2 CYBERTAX DEFINITION

Cybertax encompasses all resources required to provide and prove cybersecurity. This includes prevention, monitoring, remediation, improvements, and proving. It includes all the due diligence to select technology products and services that will improve your cybersecurity posture or, at a minimum, cause no harm. It includes the time and effort to design, implement, and monitor secure business processes. It also includes the resources required to monitor the security of your third-party providers.

Proving is an underappreciated aspect of cybertax. This includes all assessments by business partners, auditors, and regulators. It includes the cybersecurity team scrambling to answer leadership questions based upon an article in the *Wall Street Journal* or a published security incident at a competitor. In effect, it's a tax on top of the cybertax. Proving drains resources from doing, further complicating the efficient and effective deployment of cybersecurity resources.

Cybertax also includes business decisions compromised by cybersecurity considerations. For example, cybersecurity is required for all organizations, large and small. Cybertax is unavoidable; there are no cybertax-free zones. The technologies that support ubiquitous access for permissioned users and systems can be exploited by malicious actors to achieve their goals. As the internet of things (IoT) expands, so does the surface area for cybersecurity attacks beyond traditional computer systems. For those of you who see good cybersecurity as a positive attribute for an organization, we agree that cybersecurity is an acceptable way to differentiate your organization from your competitors. That said, managing the efficiency and effectiveness of resources applied to cybersecurity is imperative for any organization. Viewing cybersecurity through the cybertax lens provides an effective way for non-cybersecurity experts in leadership to manage and govern cybersecurity in their organizations. Cybertax has nothing to do with the traditional compulsory contribution of revenue to a government entity.

Cybertax is the percentage of effort and resources used to prove cybersecurity posture to others (partners, regulators, auditors), which takes effort away from providing cybersecurity capability. Time spent **proving** cybersecurity posture to auditors, regulators, business partners and others takes time away from **doing** cybersecurity. This factor will have a disproportionate effect on the score. A high cybertax score is extremely detrimental to cybersecurity capability. Your cybertax goal, as with other forms of taxation, is to minimize and optimize this tax.

## 1.3 CYBERTAX AND ZERO TRUST

Zero Trust is one of the more recent concepts that influence how organizations address cybersecurity. It used to be that there were aspects of your technology, employees, and key vendors that were vetted and "trusted" to use your technology resources and data properly. This has been replaced by Zero Trust, which is similar to the Reagan-era quote, "Trust but verify." Systems and humans are permissioned in your organization to carry out various activities that benefit the organization, its customers, and stakeholders. Technology systems are now layered on top to monitor for anomalous behavior and notify or stop the unexpected behavior. We've all read news stories where an employee who could only process dozens of accounts or files accessed and copied millions of records for unintended and malicious purpose. Zero Trust works hand in hand with cybertax to focus an organization's efforts on the most effective use of cybersecurity resources.

This book provides a Zero Trust model for how to engage, direct, and challenge your cybersecurity team much like you would your sales, revenue, or human resources function.

## 1.4 CHAPTER SUMMARY

In this chapter, we have defined what cybertax is and why executives, board members, and others with responsibility for or oversight over security should be concerned. Most importantly, we have stated that a high cybertax score is extremely detrimental to cybersecurity capability. In the following chapters we will describe the things that contribute to cybertax and what you can do about it.

# Chapter 2

# Cybertax Management

## 2.1 INTRODUCTION

Cybersecurity is the last frontier of executive suite risk management. Managing financials, sales, human capital, competition, and other significant business drivers, leadership has access to real-time tools and analytics that enable it to manage risks and key decisions with access to valuable information. These critical aspects risk management are highly correlated drivers of organization survival and success.

The lack of cybersecurity metrics and insights is the big outlier for the portfolio of enterprise risks. There is no Salesforce.com-like dashboard and insights for leadership to probe and challenge the best way to improve an organization's cybersecurity posture and reduce the likelihood of a significant cybersecurity event. In addition, the language of cybersecurity might as well be a foreign language to most business executives. Terms like bots, intrusions, malware, script kitties, and many others have little correlation with business activity. It's imperative to push your cybersecurity leadership to deliver reports and statistics in a business context beyond the "it's a bad world and the sky is falling." Cybersecurity remains an outlier when you correlate the risk to the tools and metrics available to executive leadership in the C-suite and the board of directors. There is a chasm between how current tools monitor and measure cybersecurity and the correlation with business and organization risk.

It's imperative that your cybersecurity leadership be familiar with how the business works, what its critical assets and relationships are, and how the business drives value. Many chief information security officers (CISOs) have little or no knowledge when it comes to understanding your front-, middle-, and back-office operations. Get them educated!

In an interconnected world, the definition of the enterprise must be expanded to the meta-enterprise. The meta-enterprise is not to be confused with the social media and virtual reality company. We define the meta-enterprise as the core enterprise along with vendors, accountants, bankers, law firms, consulting firms, and other support entities that make up the meta-enterprise. The meta-enterprise can also include key customers that have access to your information systems. All of these outside entities hold sensitive information, contribute to key business functions, and have electronic connections to the core enterprise. When driving cybersecurity governance, you must drive decisions and goals of your meta-enterprise.

Zero Trust is the latest concept influencing cybersecurity programs. Essentially, Zero Trust is based on the principle that nothing is implicitly trusted. For example, just because a user has permission to access particular data, the context of the usage needs to be analyzed beyond the initial permission to allow this data access and manipulation. As you can imagine, Zero Trust is another form of cybertax. Zero Trust is an added layer of permissioning and monitoring key business events, resources, and transactions. Zero Trust is an added cost (cybertax) on critical business events.

## 2.2 CYBERTAX METRICS AND MEASUREMENT

### 2.2.1 The Seven C's Intro

We developed the Seven C's to drive measuring and reporting cybersecurity posture in business terms and context. We also use the Seven C's to understand how business decisions impact your cybersecurity posture and cybertax. Although CISOs are typically responsible for all aspects of cybersecurity, they are largely the victim of business decisions that increase the cybertax. CISOs rarely have input into mergers, new products, new vendors, and even some technology decisions, yet they are responsible for protecting it all. The Seven C's is a framework designed to inform business leadership of the cybersecurity impact of their business decisions. The Seven C's are as follows:

1. **Complexity**—All aspects of complexity, including business, location, vendors, technology, and regulatory. Take, for example, laptop PCs. Limited complexity is a single laptop standard where extreme complexity is allowing any PC that can run the required business software. Obviously, it's easier to design a cybersecurity program around a single PC standard than one designed to protect nearly all PCs. The same is true of other business decisions that increase or limit business and technical complexity.

   Complexity is ever increasing and contributing to your organization's cybertax. Beyond PCs and smartphones, consider the increase in "smart" devices proliferating across enterprises in all industries. These connected devices, although helpful when they work, expand the surface area of attack for threat actors.

2. **Capability**—The reasonable throughput that the cybersecurity team can process. Capability is the measure of the organization's ability to address cybersecurity issues and responsibilities proactively and reactively. This is measured against internal policy goals as well as relative to peers. Capability factors include the following:
   - Technology footprint
   - Ability of the cybersecurity team to effectively use the technology
   - Skills and industry knowledge of the cybersecurity team
   - Cybersecurity interaction with organization leadership

7

Capability has its own tax, **proving**, which will increase the overall tax proportionate to the level of proving provided by the cybersecurity team. Proving is the percentage of effort and resources used to prove cybersecurity posture to others (e.g., partners, regulators, auditors), which takes effort away from providing cybersecurity capability. Time spent **proving** cybersecurity posture to auditors, regulators, business partners, and others takes time away from **doing** cybersecurity. This factor will have a disproportionate effect on the score. A high **proving** score is detrimental to cybersecurity capability as it diverts resources from **doing**.

A perfect capability score does not mean the organization's cybersecurity posture is perfect; it merely indicates that the resources are aligned well to deliver effective cybersecurity services. No organization is immune to cybersecurity incidents.

3. **Competency**—How effective the organization is in finding, fixing, and remediating cybersecurity events. This measures the effective execution of cybersecurity across the organization. Good cybersecurity can be measured, for example, in the following ways:

   - Are we finding new issues and not repeating others?
   - Are we finding issues sooner?
   - Are we spending more time providing cybersecurity rather than proving it to others?

   Competency measure factors such as these and others determine both absolute competency and the trend and velocity of the trend over time. This information informs leadership as to areas of good cybersecurity competency and those areas requiring leadership attention.

4. **Comparison**—How does our organization compare to peers in cybersecurity. Although each organization must determine their own cybersecurity goals and capabilities,

it's often helpful to understand how one's organization compares to similar organizations. Comparison data delivers valuable reference information.

5. **Conceptualization**—Modeling how business and technology decisions will impact the cybertax. Using the *what if* capability of CYBERPHOS, organizations can analyze and understand how changes in one area will impact the overall cybersecurity posture score. This method provides factors that can be adjusted to determine the impact of potential changes or improvements. For example, a company moving from a divergent set of laptops to a single laptop standard would see their complexity score reduce and their cybersecurity posture increase. This feature can also be used to analyze the impact of an acquisition or divestiture.

6. **Cost**—All costs related to cybersecurity, including outside assessments and regulatory review and input. Coupled with the CYBERPHOS conceptualization tool, organizations can understand the approximate cost of investments that could reduce complexity, improve capabilities, and increase data frequency to drive improved competency. Cost is determined both in dollars and calendar time. Using the laptop example above, this tool calculates the total cost of changing from a heterogeneous population of laptops to a homogeneous state. This tool comes with a standard set of cost metrics that can be customized by a particular organization.

7. **Continuous**—For the Seven C's to be effective, measures must be used frequently to spot negative trends early. Unlike annual assessments that are conducted at a specific point in time, this method relies on information that is frequently updated from daily to near real-time (NRT), so that it can more accurately communicate trends and velocity of change in key factors of cybersecurity risk. Frequent information updates also reduce the human bias found in traditional cybersecurity assessments.

The Seven C's method does not determine the appropriate amount of risk an organization should tolerate, but it does help leadership understand key factors influencing their organization's cybersecurity risk and how to improve its cybersecurity posture. Similar to other key risks, leadership must apply resources to deliver a risk level appropriate for the organization and its partners and customers.

This method highlights factors influencing cybersecurity complexity, capability, and competency. Not only will this method provide an absolute and peer-relevant complexity score, but it will also indicate which factors influence the score in impact order. This enables leadership to focus on issues that impact and improve cybersecurity posture. This is driven by alerts built into the tool that highlight areas requiring leadership's attention.

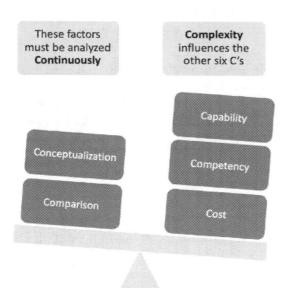

## The Seven C's

**Figure 2.1   The Seven C's**

The Seven C's method (see Figure 2.1) also monitors trends, both positive and negative, so leadership can assess the organization's ability to find and respond to the ever-changing spectrum of cybersecurity threats. For example, a trend highlighting that similar cybersecurity exploits are increasing point to an organization that is ineffective at learning from previous exploits and unable to develop a wholistic solution. A trend demonstrating that the organization is finding cybersecurity incidents faster highlights an improving aspect of competency.

## 2.2.2 How to Measure

Measuring the Seven C's method must be similar to other key business measures: events, costs, effectiveness, and trends. You want these events categorized by high, medium, and low impact. We see too many CISOs try to report meaningless, low-impact statistics—for example, how many million times a day an unauthorized system tries to connect to your organization in order to prove their importance or worth to the organization. Those network pings are handled by all well-configured network hardware and software and are, thus, low impact.

## 2.2.3 How to Monitor

The Seven C's believes that monitoring key aspects of cybersecurity should be frequent, like other aspects of business. It's surprising how many businesses still rely on annual or semiannual assessments to understand their cybersecurity program and posture. These assessments are expensive, rely on human and not scientific inputs, and drain time away from your best cybersecurity resources. We know because we've conducted many of these assessments, which have proven to be of limited value but provide a feeling of "comfort," especially when delivered by a large accounting firm.

A business does not look at its financials once a year after a financial audit. It has systems and metrics that are tracked daily, weekly, and monthly. The same principle should be applied to cybersecurity metrics and trends.

## 2.2.4 Culture—Leadership

The largest department of any organization is the cybersecurity department. That's because every employee, vendor, regulator, and customer can behave in ways that improves or harms your cybersecurity posture. When it comes to cybersecurity policies and rules, we favor fewer rules and policies that are ruthlessly enforced. This includes the C-suite and the board of directors—no exceptions! Many organizations have extensive security policies, but they lack the resources or will to enforce them. The worst thing you can do is to have a policy that is not monitored or enforced.

## 2.2.5 Culture—Make New Mistakes

Cybersecurity is an anathema to business leadership because no amount of time or money will drive the risk to zero. Even the most capable organizations are susceptible to a cybersecurity event. Given this reality you should tolerate **making new mistakes** and discourage **repeating mistakes.** Let us explain. When capturing a cybersecurity event, a critical aspect of the event should be whether it is new—something we've never seen before or one of a number of events we've captured in the past. Leadership should be more tolerant of new mistakes and less tolerant of repeating mistakes. This concept is applied to manufacturing, finance, and human resources, so why not cybersecurity as well?

The other aspect of **make new mistakes** is to capture and compare the harm after an incident. The goal should be to reduce the impact over time from both new and repeated mistakes. For example, if you have a data breach and you lose one million records, subsequent breaches should see a reduction in the amount of damage.

We realize that you are in some ways measuring damage, but as with other domains, limiting damage and getting better at catching damage should be monitored and rewarded.

## 2.3 CYBERTAX MANAGEMENT

### 2.3.1 Using the Key Metrics

The Seven C's method has highlighted vital aspects and trends to track and analyze. The Seven C's forces a business to track not simply cybersecurity metrics but the key business decisions that impact delivering effective cybersecurity as well. It's important for business leaders to own their contribution to cybersecurity effectiveness as well as holding the cybersecurity function accountable for its mission.

### 2.3.2 Directing Goals

Cybersecurity goals should be driven by business objectives and outcomes. Cybersecurity goals should be focused on protecting key business assets, limiting regulatory intrusion, and driving safe, secure outcomes for all stakeholders. Using the Seven C's model should drive trends and insights that empower leadership to direct goals as they do in other management domains.

### 2.3.3 Driving Outcomes

Outcomes should focus on reducing complexity, driving capability efficiency, and reducing the cybertax—all in the name of improving cybersecurity posture. Business decisions should consider their impact on cybersecurity and the outcome. Every organization has cybersecurity incidents. Drive towards finding these issues sooner and, if not preventing the incident, reducing the impact of the incident and not repeating the same mistakes.

### 2.3.4 Do More/Do Less

Inevitably, your security organization wants to do more, buy more tools and services, hire more resources, use third parties to improve aspects of the cybersecurity program, or respond to changes in the business. New adversaries, products, geographies, and acquisitions may influence the need to increase cybersecurity efforts. We've been involved in many of these discussions. What is rarely discussed is what we will do less or spend less on.

In other aspects of the business governance, this is a normal discussion—for example, a decision to devote more resources to R&D and less on marketing. Spending more to implement Zero Trust principles may mean spending less on protecting the endpoints of your enterprise. The following key principles should drive Do More/Do Less:

1. Reduce business complexity when driving business decisions and goals. Reducing business and technical complexity makes it easier for your cybersecurity team to focus and deliver a better cybersecurity posture. Reducing complexity reduces the cybertax.

2. Don't pay premium prices for commodity services. At one time, antivirus, endpoint protection, firewalls, and many other aspects of a cybersecurity architecture were novel and provided innovative protection. Today, these products are necessary but insufficient to provide a good cybersecurity posture. It's important that your cybersecurity program recognizes when to pay premium versus commodity pricing for the many products and services required for a good cybersecurity program. Paying premium prices for commodity products increases the cybertax.

3. Limit spending on threat intelligence. Spending resources on threat intelligence is necessary for a nation-state; it's rarely beneficial for a corporation. Although there is useful intelligence to enable your network team to block traffic from known harmful network addresses (IPs), it's

a unicorn event to have a bad actor announce that they will attack your organization in this way on this date. Many cybersecurity professionals gained their knowledge in government service where threat intelligence is essential. Your resources are better spent training these resources on how the business works.

4. Learn the business. In our travels, it's always surprising how many CISOs are not well versed in how the business operates and succeeds. Spending time and effort to train the CISO team on these aspects will yield significant dividends for your organization.

5. Plan for bad events. All organizations will have negative cybersecurity events. Good organizations plan for these events and have readiness plans in place, as opposed to scrambling and reacting after the incident is discovered. Although an action plan will never be 100 percent accurate, it's better to start with a remediation plan that uses a flexible framework that can be adapted to new and unforeseen circumstances.

## 2.4 SUMMARY

It's time to take the mystery out of cybersecurity and monitor and manage it like other key enterprise risks. Using the Seven C's method, your organization can better understand, monitor, and manage cybersecurity risk.

In this chapter, we described the key aspects of cybertax metrics and measurement. We outlined the Seven C's, which we developed to measure and report cybersecurity posture in business terms and context. We also described how to use the Seven C's to measure and monitor cybersecurity risk as well as corporate culture's effect on the process. The last part of the chapter focused on cybertax management, using key metrics, directing goals and outcomes, and the application of the principles of "Do More/Do Less" as key elements of the management process.

# Chapter 3

# Cybertax Efficiency

## 3.1 INTRODUCTION

As stated in Chapter 1, cybertax encompasses all resources required to provide and prove cybersecurity. This includes prevention, monitoring, remediation, improvements, and proving. It includes all the due diligence to select technology products and services that will improve your cybersecurity posture or, at a minimum, cause no harm. It includes the time and effort to design, implement, monitor, and improve secure business processes. It also includes the resources required to monitor the security of your third-party providers, your meta-enterprise. In this chapter, we discuss how to optimize cybertax efficiency and effectiveness.

## 3.2 DRIVING EFFICIENCY

Over the last decade or so, significant technological advancements have resulted in improved operational efficiencies for cybersecurity. Unfortunately, threat actors continue to advance their capabilities to compromise technology and humans to gain access to their targeted assets. In addition, the surface area of attack is increasing faster than tools to protect and manage their new technology assets. Think of the proliferation of smart devices in your home. Now, project that to your enterprise and you can conceptualize the attack surface area of your organization.

Many organizations continue to rely on "check box" approaches to security compliance and efficiencies: Does yours? In addition, vendor point solutions continue to solve narrow problems, as opposed to building a comprehensive and mature cybersecurity program. Part of evaluating cybertax is to identify these types of insufficiencies and then align security needs with larger business goals, create overall solutions that can accomplish objectives in multiple areas rather than point solutions, improve your work-flows, and most importantly, reduce the cost and overhead of security within your organization. Some of the key areas that are critical for more economic and efficient cybersecurity programs that are evaluated as part of the cybertax assessment include asset inventory; vulnerability assessment; threat and vulnerability management; network detection and response; threat intelligence; security information and event management (SIEM); governance, risk, and compliance (GRC); and ticketing (security orchestration). The online Balbix™ whitepaper,[1] identifies these 8 key areas, as delineated below:

- **Asset Inventory:** Assets are resources that a company uses to run its business, produce items, or deliver a service. The primary goal of asset management is keeping track of the company's assets. Good asset management should always lead to improved asset performance, fewer safety incidents, improved business productivity, and, most importantly, lower operating costs. Asset inventory should also include vendor solutions connected to your organization, including cloud services and Software as a Service (SaaS).

  Organizational assets constantly being added and retired, which can result in inaccurate inventory, makes managing compliance and cyber-risk very difficult.[2]

- **Vulnerability Assessment:** A vulnerability assessment is the process of identifying, quantifying, and prioritizing the vulner-abilities in a system or software. Vulnerability assessments are one of the ways that IT teams determine the overall security of a business's systems, which determines where technological vulnerabilities are and how they need to be dealt with. Without vulnerability assessments, businesses may leave themselves open to cyber attacks and a variety of other security issues that can erode public confidence and result in financial issues for the parent company. Vulnerability assessments apply to technology, humans, vendors, and service providers.

Highly qualified security talent is required to analyze the collection of massive outputs from threat and vulnerability tools before any action can be taken. Typically, traditional scanning solutions are unable to discern levels of mission criticality between assets, thus requiring human skill and analysis to do so.[3]

- **Threat and Vulnerability Management:** Vulnerability management is the practice of identifying, classifying, remediating, and mitigating weaknesses in an IT environment. It also includes discovery, reporting, prioritization, and response to vulnerabilities in your network.[4] Operationally, it includes an ongoing process that includes proactive asset discovery, continuous monitoring, mitigation, remediation, and defense tactics to protect your organization from cyber risk.

  Prioritization of vulnerability capabilities allows you to begin threat and vulnerability management, base your patching activities on business risk, and align your team's efforts with overall business objectives. Another solution beyond your scanning tool is typically required for prioritization, adding to an organization's yearly budget and workload.[5]

- **Network Detection and Response:** Network detection and response solutions use a combination of non–signature-based advanced analytical techniques such as machine learning to detect suspicious network activity. These solutions may utilize threat intelligence from inside and outside of the organization and are used to help detect potential threats within network traffic. This enables the security team to respond to anomalous or malicious traffic and threats.

  Although reactive security measures have become the norm with the ever-expanding attack surfaces and potential entry points, defaulting and overreliance on reactive technology and practices is a flawed approach. Organizations should shift their focus to proactive measures for solid cybersecurity hygiene and vetting out weaknesses across all assets, applications, and users prior to an event as an efficient and less resource-intensive practice. Continuous monitoring of your network and a response plan are critical in today's evolving threat environment.[6]

- **Threat Intelligence:** Threat intelligence, or cyber threat intelligence, is data that is collected, processed, and analyzed to understand a threat actor's motives, targets, and attack behaviors. This, in turn, leads to an understanding of the threats that have, will, or are currently targeting the organization and how to detect and stop those attacks. Most importantly, this information is used to prepare for, prevent, and identify cyber threats.

  As the threat landscape evolves exponentially, teams are continually challenged to understand the subset of vulnerabilities that are being actively exploited by attackers. Tools are used to manage and process the potentially thousands of sources of threat intelligence in order to rank and prioritize the information that helps uncover critical, exploitable vulnerabilities. Common Vulnerabilities and Exposures (CVEs) are used by software companies to give customers maximum transparency to vulnerabilities in software they have purchased.[7]

  It is a unicorn event that threat intelligence will alert you to a specific attack at a time in the future. The threat intelligence industry was launched off similar services designed to protect nation-states from logical and physical attacks. There are limited benefits from threat intelligence services. Therefore, do not expect them to keep you from harm.

- **Security Information and Event Management (SIEM):** SIEM is a security solution that helps organizations recognize potential security threats and vulnerabilities before they have a chance to disrupt business operations. It combines security information management (SIM) and security event management (SEM) to provide real-time monitoring and analysis of events as well as tracking and logging of security data for compliance or auditing purposes. It has become an invaluable tool for security operation centers (SOCs) automating many of the manual processes associated with threat detection and incident response.

Similar to Network Detection and Response, SIEM has become a focal point for acting on security intelligence and making sense of overwhelming swaths of vulnerability data. SIEM tools typically pull data from other mitigating controls, network devices, servers, and domain controllers and aim to surface meaningful anomalies for necessary action.[8]

- **Governance, Risk, and Compliance (GRC):** GRC refers to all the capabilities that integrate governance, management, and assurance of performance, risk and compliance activities. The goal is to unify and align an organization's approach to risk management and regulatory compliance. Strengthening and building acceptance of these processes helps improve business performance and enhance decision making within corporate governance boards.

  The key to effective GRC management is an accurate and up-to-date inventory of all your enterprise's data, categorized by departments and/or risk owners. You also need to know which assets are holding highly sensitive information, such as customer personal identifiable information (PII) or intellectual property. The accuracy of your data governance drives the high-level understanding of risk and resource allocation. Mapping these items of risk toward an acceptable framework adopted by the business is how many decisions are being made.[9]

- **Security Orchestration and Ticketing:** Security orchestration is a method of connecting and integrating your systems, security tools, and processes. It maximizes the use of automation to get the most value out of your people, processes, and tools.

Having all the information in one place, with streamlined security processes, enhances the security team's decision-making ability and response time to security incidents. Security Operation Centers (SOCs) optimize their ticketing systems to streamline assessments, automate response plans, and provide comprehensive reporting. Ideally, SOCs will integrate their security orchestration and ticketing systems.

Security teams require clear risk insights delivered to specific owners with context and prioritization by severity. These insights are only valuable if they are both accurate and acted on appropriately, with little delay. Proper security orchestration and ticketing will enable security teams to align their efforts efficiently with results.[10]

The metrics and reporting of the CYBERPHOS platform (see Chapter 6) facilitates the creation of a roadmap to improve the maturity and efficiency of your cybersecurity program. This is derived from the evaluation of cybertax to include those items described above. A constant view of the health of your organization's cybersecurity posture will ensure that the senior executives and board of directors (BoD) are holding the security team and other groups accountable for all cybersecurity risks that can be detrimental to the company's business and its responsibilities to its customers. Automation, consolidation of data, and streamlined and business-relevant security reporting are elements that help improve the efficiency based on the risks identified during cybertax evaluation.

## 3.3 DRIVING EFFECTIVENESS

Evaluating cybertax is key to knowing whether you are measuring the right things. If you are not measuring the value and effectiveness of your cybersecurity efforts, you are flying blind and have no idea if your cybersecurity projects and program are effective. Even those security programs that do generate and provide data metrics to executives typically don't get their reports read. This is generally because the security group is not reporting security effectiveness from a business-impact perspective and not evaluating risk versus impact.

Many CISOs have little or no interaction with the audiences to whom they report. As a result, they are guessing at what their audiences need and miss the mark when attempting to provide ongoing management reporting on topics such as information security effectiveness, organizational risk, and information security arrangements. Combining the cybertax evaluation methodology with the CYBERPHOS reporting platform provides for a common language from a business-risk perspective that enhances the effectiveness of your security program. If the business executives and BoD don't know or understand what you're doing, how can they help you? They may make some assumptions about what you're doing and could be completely wrong. By realigning this process to the business, it's no longer the CISO's problem, it's the business's problem as to whether they want to find the funding for or support the problem. Addressing cyber risk as a cybertax issue in business terms significantly increases effectiveness because it ensures that the right conversations are happening with the right people. This results in getting the right data calibrated and supported by the right business owners for the right audiences that will understand the business context and key priorities of the organization's cyber risk.

## 3.4 REWARDING PROGRESS

As the cyber threat environment continues to evolve rapidly, with new threats emerging all the time, cybersecurity issues have become a top concern of C-suite executives and board members. The scale of attacks has also caught the attention and concern of shareholders, the media, customers, and regulators.

Proper evaluation of cybertax will reward an organization through the identification of areas of security deficiencies that can then be addressed to achieve programmatic efficiencies and effectiveness. Some of the rewards that an organization will achieve from progressing through this process include:

- Recognition of the need for innovation to keep defenses strong and to keep pace with evolving needs
- Involving cybersecurity proactively when making business decisions that will impact the scope and complexity of your cybersecurity function
- The ability to quickly adopt, adapt, and improve security management measures, such as the use of metrics, benchmarking, risk-management procedures, and ongoing communication with the C-suite and the BoD
- Providing an improved mechanism for the CISO to have a business-oriented direct channel to the CEO and BoD to facilitate the improvement of security strategy and initiatives, and better communication in the case of a serious security incident
- Establishment of a strong relationship among the CISO, the CEO, and the BoD rather than a relationship that is filtered through several levels of operational management
- Facilitating business-oriented corporate-wide security disaster recovery and business continuity management practices rather than those that rely solely on IT-focused security policies and standard operating procedures
- Recognition that security threats—in particular, major breaches—go beyond monetary losses and endanger corporate reputation and brand value
- Alignment of the security strategy with the organization's business goals
- Senior management and BoD awareness of a business-oriented security strategy and a view to the outcomes that are (or are not) being achieved
- A view to the profitability and risk of every security programmatic effort to avoid costly mistakes

## 3.5 SUMMARY

Cybertax efficiency is the percentage of effort and resources used to prove cybersecurity posture to others. Time spent proving cybersecurity posture to auditors, regulators, business partners, and others takes effort away from providing cybersecurity capability. In this chapter, we have described the optimization, efficiency, and effectiveness of dealing with cybertax.

## REFERENCES

1. Bradford, N. (2020, July 8). 8 Key Areas to Improve Cybersecurity Efficiency. Blog. Retrieved from https://www.balbix.com/blog/8-key-areas-to-improve-cybersecurity-efficiency/
2. Ibid.
3. Ibid.
4. Coresecurity. (2022). Vulnerability Management Program. Retrieved from https://www.coresecurity.com/threat-detection/vulnerability-management-program
5. Bradford, N. (2020, July 8). 8 Key Areas to Improve Cybersecurity Efficiency. Blog. Retrieved from https://www.balbix.com/blog/8-key-areas-to-improve-cybersecurity-efficiency/
6. Ibid.
7. Ibid.
8. Bradford, N. (2020, July 8). 8 Key Areas to Improve Cybersecurity Efficiency. Blog. Retrieved from https://www.balbix.com/blog/8-key-areas-to-improve-cybersecurity-efficiency/
9. Ibid.
10. Ibid.

# Chapter 4

# Know Your Adversary

## 4.1 INTRODUCTION

As part of the CYBERPHOS cybertax assessment, we provide you with an overview of what your security and/or risk officer should be telling you. Attacks are not necessarily effective because they are sophisticated but rather because they take advantage existing vulnerabilities that are easy to exploit and considered low-hanging fruit—for example, software that is not up to date (unpatched), employees that open malicious emails disguised as something benign, and obtaining access through a vendor that is less secure than your enterprise. Knowledge of the threat actors and their attack and exploitation methodologies are key to understanding the cybersecurity risk in your organization.

Cybersecurity is a significant risk for every organization. Cybercriminals are organized, weaponized, and sophisticated. The proliferation of connected devices and organizations increase the surface area of attack for threat actors. The information and language chasm between the practitioners of cybersecurity and corporate leadership is ever increasing, making it more difficult for leadership to govern cybersecurity. To date, boards of directors, C-suite executives, and private equity firms have lacked business-driven tools to manage this risk like other key business risks, such as financial, growth, and sales. Leadership needs a business language tool to bridge this chasm to effectively manage cybersecurity risks.

There are many cybersecurity frameworks and assessments that are derived from the ISO® 27001 standards. These assessments are useful for cybersecurity practitioners but do little to help leadership understand and manage cybersecurity risk. Leadership in this context is defined as the key business owners, C-suite executives, and the board of directors. These frameworks do little to combine business complexity and cybersecurity capability into a competency score that guides leadership attention, issue probing, and governance for the cybersecurity team and its services.

The other significant gap in the current frameworks is that they measure cybersecurity effectiveness as a point-in-time exercise, typically annually. Every other significant risk to the organization is measured and monitored with near real-time (NRT) information and metrics. Think of sales, growth, finances, human resources, and supply chain, all of which are measured, monitored, and analyzed with NRT information. Why is cybersecurity risk, which is potentially unlimited, measured and governed infrequently?

Organizations strive to improve their cybersecurity posture in a world in which cybersecurity threats and vectors are constantly evolving. Think of cybersecurity posture as the overall cybersecurity competency score. Infrequent measurements of cybersecurity risk are inadequate in a world where the threat actors operate in real time.

## 4.2 CYBERSECURITY RISK

All organizations have cybersecurity risks within their enterprise and their larger, connected meta-enterprise, which includes connections to vendors, customers, regulators, and other providers. Most organizations use some combination of NIST's *Framework for Improving Critical Infrastructure Cybersecurity*, ISO 27001&2 security guidelines, and Center for Internet Security (CIS) tools to drive annual assessments of cybersecurity posture. These assessments are useful to chief information security officers (CISOs) for understanding the strengths and weaknesses of their cybersecurity program but provide few insights for leadership charged with managing all organization significant risks, including cybersecurity risk.

## 4.3 CYBERSECURITY THREATS

Even though cyber is virtualized and distributed, its physical inter-connection with communication and data distribution systems can be greatly impacted by disrupting cyber assets that may or may not be within the borders of that country, such as satellites, switches in bordering countries, provider networks, and myriad other computer services. This can also be true for systems such as those used for power distribution, water services, or emergency services. A cyber weapon could be constructed that renders military aircraft ineffective or disrupts targeting on the navigation systems of tanks or ground-to-air missile systems. In fact, electronic warfare systems have done this for decades. The means, methodology, and potential anonymity of an attack of this nature would be a few of the differences that distinguish a cyberattack from a conventional warfare attack. The way a cyber attack impacts a cyber asset will materialize in some manner directly or indirectly in the physical world. Cyberwarfare is a theater of war, and it will be shared with other theaters of war in the physical domain in future battles.

The cyber world is difficult to envision because of its virtual nature and scope. It is not entirely virtual however. It is integrated with the physical world through data centers, servers, routers, switches, cables, modems, communication towers, PCs, mobile devices, keyboards, printers, and storage devices.

Cyber is virtual, ubiquitous, and interconnected. It's more than just the Internet and the cloud. It is a complex network of digital systems interacting with other systems and transporting information that plays an increasingly critical role in how humans live, survive, and function. Due to its criticality, cyber has high value and is integral to our survival. Because it can be destroyed, it means that there are corresponding weapons and methodologies to deliver that destruction. This methodology and its associated weaponry are cyber warfare and the best defense against it is a good offense.

The days of the "script kiddies" or other individuals leaning towards malcontent on the Internet or doing joyriding hacks into corporate or government systems being our primary perceived threat are long gone and have perhaps been gone for over a decade or two, but the perception lingers. In today's environment we have well-organized crime organizations and nation-states who use tactics for plausible deniability that are silently infecting mobile devices, PCs, and servers for financial gain. Some of the efforts of these groups may include stealing money, collecting and stealing data (e.g., intellectual property [IP], industrial espionage, personal information), supporting terrorism (e.g., attacks on SCADA, the Internet, or governmental infrastructure), and blackmailing corporations, organizations, and individuals. These efforts are made easier because IT organizations are no longer orderly and compartmentalized but rather have become an obscured matrix of structures. Network boundaries make it much easier to hide and navigate around traditional secure defenses. Malware has evolved to the point that it can quickly be adapted to any cybercriminal business models.

Whether or not the perpetrator is organized crime or a nation-state stealing intellectual property and conducting espionage to ensure the financial competitiveness of their key industries in the global market, a key tenet to being effective in cybersecurity and defense planning is to follow the money. In order to follow the money, law enforcement must be empowered to succeed. International laws must exist to oversee conduct on the Internet. Cutting-edge technologies that can assist in the efforts to follow the money must also be developed and approved for use globally in order to support law enforcement efforts in this cause.

Anywhere that money or data that is worth money is found, you will also find those who will try to scam it away from those that have it. The common practice of tricking people into giving away financial information indicates a trend that more security threats will likely come in the virtual world. Security experts say that threats to virtual economies are now rivals to threats to real economies, in part because the virtual economies are not as regulated and consequently don't provide the same kind of protections or fail-safe controls. Phishing scams, malware, data loss—many threats abound, but security professionals dispute exactly what constitutes the most serious security threat. Almost all sources agree that over the past two to three years, cybercriminals have become incredibly professional and evermore sophisticated in their tactics. What was once about bragging rights is now about high-stake payoffs and illegitimately gained proceeds obtained by large-scale Internet fraud and infiltration.

It's worth noting that in the physical world as well as the virtual world there is no return on investment (ROI) on hate. Terrorists attack innocent targets; nation-states invade each other; and nation-states focus their offensive cyber capabilities on other nation-states, corporations, and individuals. The goals of these entities are rarely economic but rather to lash out against something they dislike, causing chaos and harm. North Korea's attack on the Sony Corporation® was triggered by the embarrassing portrayal of their Supreme Leader in the movie "The Interview."

Across the board, attacks are becoming more targeted, honing in on individuals with specific and personal demographic information. Experts say that instead of just credit cards and bank account information, they're going for everything—any and all information that can be used to create an identity. From there, attackers will either use the data or sell it on the black market to someone who will.

As information systems have become tightly connected to many large corporations, either directly or indirectly, the distinction between a civilian target and a military target may become blurred. From a cyber perspective, corporations may be looked upon as legitimate targets. Given that information transfer in civilian society is critical for it to function, a cyber weapon could have a devastating effect when used against these targets. Cyber weapons are also a preferred weapon of choice in a world where western nations prefer high-technology warfare, with the absence of or limitation of casualties.

## 4.3.1 Threat Actors: The Dark Side of a Connected World

Although the Internet and its associated connectivity have become advantageous and indispensable to both the business world and public sector, there is also a dark side filled with various threat actors. Both the intent and capabilities of the different categories of threat actors will vary considerably. We have divided these into seven categories: nation-states, proxies for nation-states, criminal organizations, competitors, employee sabotage, and malicious hackers.

### 4.3.1.1 Nation-States

Hackers are no longer working in solitary conditions and are predominantly members of organized crime groups who are also following the money. Cybercrime is truly without borders and shows tremendous returns on investments. These attacks can range from physical destruction, to electronic theft, to the large-scale crashing of critical information systems such as an entire global system to subcomponents of a national infrastructure. These attacks could be from isolated individuals (amateurs, hackers, and crackers), organized groups (organized crime, special interest groups/activists, and terrorists), commercial competitors, or even by state actors themselves.

Hackers normally possess greater technical knowledge than amateurs. These individuals also present a deeper knowledge of system complexities and reflect the intention to violate the security mechanisms of networks and information systems. Crackers, also known as benevolent hackers can be at risk because they can be an attractive asset for political dissidents and activists who may want to use their skills to gain visibility to political messages and social or special-interest views.

Traditional command and control structures may not be adequate to deal with new forms of cyber war, which may be transparent to current security systems or may come from new and unanticipated sources and directions. One of the major challenges faced by large global corporations and those managing the security of critical national infrastructures is the identification and health monitoring of the key elements of command and control functions that fall within the realm of cyberspace to provide an advanced warning of aggression or exploitation. This can include global corporate networks, government networks, critical communication nodes, national-level power, financial networks, health networks, selected media outlets, and vital networks that are components of a national infrastructure.

The technologies that are used for cyber warfare or cybercrime may also bypass controls that have been put in place internationally and regionally to prevent the spread and use of other types of weapons of mass destruction. Groups that previously did not have access to any form of strategic weaponry can now have access to cyber weapons and the associated leverage they provide to relatively small groups or individuals.

Private corporations have become dependent on the Internet and the cloud to conduct business on a global scale. As such, corporations and their subsidiaries are being seen as non-state or meta-state entities and, therefore, are targets of aggression in their own right. In many cases, they have also converged with the military and industrial complexes of their respective home states, therefore presenting an attractive target to the use of force directed toward the nation-state itself.

The globalization of competition through the use of cloud services and the Internet increases the competitive pressure on all corporations. This will likely result in the increasing use of cyber espionage and elements of cyber warfare. It is perceived as both a competitive edge and outright aggression against their competitors. Although the United States is struggling to retain its position as the dominant world power both geopolitically and financially, it is still considered number one, which makes it a prime target for those that want to upstage its influence. For those that don't have the power to challenge the United States directly, the use of non–state-identified actors in cyberspace using elements of cyber warfare is a very attractive alternative to the direct use of force. Looking at it from another perspective, the increasing dependence on cyber by developed nations leaves them vulnerable to many forms of attacks directed at computer networks and the information stored on them.

### 4.3.1.2 Proxies for Nation-States

Hackers and other individuals trained in software programming and exploiting the intricacies of computer networks can be the primary executors of these cyber attacks. Typically, those that are part of a larger group, such as organized crime groups or political activist/anarchist groups, are prime candidates to act as proxies for nation-states.

Individuals may be used to play the lone-wolf card. In either case, non-attribution is the name of the game. Within the cyber warfare arena, these teams or units are organized along nation-states. These attacks may be executed against targets in a cooperative and simultaneous manner. As more programming is subcontracted to countries outside a parent state for a corporation or from a particular government for economic reasons, the possibility of abuse by hackers, organized crime agents, and cyber terrorists in countries not necessarily allied with the country that is outsourcing such work is likely. Nation-states reconnoiter and probe to identify exploitable digital network weaknesses among potential adversaries. What better way can you think of to avoid detection or culpability than to have an organization do the work as your proxy and give you plausible deniability?

### 4.3.1.3 Criminal Organizations

The evolution of cybercrime capabilities has increased at an incredible pace over the last few years. This has incentivized and empowered smaller groups who can now purchase these capabilities at a reasonable price on the Internet. Asymmetric impacts such as controlling botnets with millions of infected hosts are now possible for small teams of cybercriminals. Whether the criminal organization's goal is monetary, access to intellectual property, or the disruption of critical systems, the rapidly evolving threat landscape presents a complex and vital challenge for national and economic security.[1]

Along with the evolution of the Internet, cybercrime has evolved from the domain of individuals and small groups to traditional organized crime syndicates and criminally minded technology professionals working together and pooling their resources and expertise. This has been largely due to the speed, convenience, and anonymity that modern technologies offer to those wanting to commit a diverse range of criminal activities. Consequently, just as brick-and mortar companies moved their enterprises to the World Wide Web (WWW) seeking new opportunities for profits, criminal enterprises are doing the same thing. The global nature of the Internet has allowed criminals to commit almost any illegal activity anywhere in the world, making it essential for all countries to adapt their domestic offline controls to cover crimes carried out in cyberspace. These activities include attacks against computer data and systems, identity theft, the distribution of child sexual abuse images, Internet auction fraud, money laundering, the penetration of online financial services, online banking theft, illicit access to intellectual property, and online extortion, as well as the deployment of viruses, botnets, and various email scams such as phishing. Organized crime groups typically have a home base in a nation that provides a safe haven, from which they conduct their transnational operations. In effect, this provides an added degree of protection against law enforcement and allows them to operate with minimal risk. The inherently transnational nature of the Internet fits perfectly into this model of activity and the effort to maximize profits within an acceptable degree of risk. In the virtual world there are no borders, a characteristic that makes it very attractive for criminal activity; yet when it comes to policing this virtual world, borders and national jurisdictions loom large—making large-scale investigation slow and tedious, at best, and impossible, at worst. Some of the more noteworthy groups are the European crime rings, state-sponsored criminal groups and proxies, U.S. domestic crime groups, and Mexican cartels.[2-4] As payoff from cybercrime grows, it is no surprise that organized crime groups seek a share in it. Cybercrime allows organized syndicates to finance their other illicit activities in addition to providing hefty profits. Criminal syndicates are involved in everything from theft to extortion, piracy, and enabling online crime in the first place. They are providing a new meaning to the "as-a-service" term. In addition to exploiting cyber infrastructure for monetary gains, they are enabling cyber attacks by providing vulnerabilities, creating tools, and offering resources to people who will pay for it. These services include selling vulnerabilities (proactively looking for them in new software products and infrastructure), creating and selling exploits for existing vulnerabilities, spam services, infrastructure (botnets, hosting), as well as malware.[5,6]

In regions of the world where cybercriminal organizations flourish, they behave much like any organization seeking talent. They recruit from the best technical universities; they offer benefits, and they pay bonuses for success. The war for talent has expanded in the criminal world, particularly where such activity is condoned and rewarded. I once heard a respected business executive refer to Chinese corporate espionage as "aggressive capitalism." Clearly, there is no stigma attached to hacking in that part of the world.

### 4.3.1.4 Competitors

Although we are primarily focused on the threat to corporations, albeit rare, cybercriminals can also be a threat actor to domestic and foreign competitors. They may hire external hackers or use their own capabilities to embarrass, disrupt, or steal from other corporations. A few examples of techniques that we have seen over the years that competitor threat actors have used include the following:

*Undercut offers from a competitor.* Individuals from a corporation may breach a database containing information belonging to the competitor. The attackers can use the information from there to undercut the offers from the competitor and use it in their sales pitches. This can be effective in all sizes of enterprises as a risk of attack from their competitors.

*Denying the competition.* Distributed denial-of-service (DDoS) attack against a competing firm as a tactic employed against competitors that rely on constant uptime to service their customers. If these attacks are timed so that they coincide with a competitive bidding process, attacks like this are very damaging for a target company.

*Obtaining competitive data.* Seeking to steal proprietary data to benefit their own product or service. Utilizing malware and maintaining persistence on a target network. A nefarious company slowly extracting proprietary data from a competitor. It is also possible that a corporation utilizes their position in industry to craft convincing social engineering emails to breach the network. This can be part of a nation-state or just an unscrupulous company that wants to gain a strategic advantage from either a military or commercial perspective, and sometimes both.

*Reputation damage.* Seek to damage the reputation of a competitor to gain the upper hand; they may be seeking to blackmail employees of the target company to turn them into malicious insiders.[7]

### 4.3.1.5 Employee Sabotage

Employee sabotage can be both inadvertent and deliberate. "Accidental" spillage of a drink on a keyboard or laptop causing it to be unusable is an example of an inadvertent employee offense. Mistakenly turning off the servers over the weekend is another. For our discussion, the primary concern is intentional sabotage. As long as people feel unjustly treated, cheated, bored, harassed, endangered, or betrayed at work, sabotage will be used as a method of achieving revenge or a twisted sense of job satisfaction. An employee also has the edge over outsiders, since they have familiarity with the corporation's computers, systems, networks, and electronic storage, which gives them the target knowledge advantage. The number of incidents of employee sabotage is believed to be much smaller than the instances of theft, but the cost of such incidents can be quite high.[8]

### 4.3.1.6 Malicious Hackers

The term "malicious hacker" refers to someone who break into computers without authorization. Malicious hackers can be outsiders or insiders. The hacker threat should be considered in terms of past and potential future damage. Although current losses due to hacker attacks constitute significantly smaller losses due to insider theft and sabotage, the hacker problem is widespread and serious. One example of malicious hacker activity is that directed against the public telephone system (which is, by the way, quite common; the targets are usually employee voice mailboxes or special "internal-only" numbers allowing free calls to company insiders). Another common method is for hackers to attempt to gather information about internal systems by using port scanners and sniffers, password attacks, DoS attacks, and various other attempts to break into publicly exposed systems such as file transfer protocol (FTP) and WWW servers. By implementing efficient firewalls and auditing/alerting mechanisms, external hackers can be thwarted. Internal hackers are extremely difficult to contend with, since they have already been granted access. However, conducting internal audits on a frequent and recurring basis will help organizations to detect these activities.

## 4.3.2 Compromise Vectors

Attack vectors are the methods cybercriminals use to gain unauthorized access to a system, while an attack surface refers to the total number of attack vectors used by an intruder to control or steal data from your network or endpoints. Vectors of attacks refer to the pathway that cyber attackers take to infiltrate your organization. In essence, an attack vector is a process or route a malicious hacker uses to reach a target or, in other words, the measures the attacker takes to conduct an attack.[9] In this section, we will be covering the main attack vectors used to compromise corporate enterprises.

### 4.3.2.1 Strategic, Tactical, and User-Specific Attacks

#### Strategic

Strategic software attacks are highly repeatable and use general targeting such as against a broad industry (military, finance, energy, etc.) or groups of individuals (politicians, executives), and they must have long-term staying power. Strategic attacks are less sophisticated in comparison to tactical threats and typically are lower in cost to develop and maintain. These types of attacks can be categorized into three major areas: espionage, criminal, and sociopolitical.[10]

In general, strategic software targets are applications that are essential to critical infrastructure functions of the government, economy, or society at large. Strategic attacks are typically planned and controlled to target information assets, including specifications, technologies, plans, capabilities, procedures, and guidelines, to gain strategic advantage. They are typically conducted by state sponsors (or by entities supported by states), organized crime, or competitors. Tactical attacks are typically random and opportunistic; they target information assets for prestige or financial reward through the use of malware, exploits, hackers, surrogates, insider threats, and chat rooms, and they are conducted by professional hackers, script kiddies, and insiders. As you can see, one of the key differentiators between tactical and strategic attacks is motive: Tactical attacks target network assets for prestige or financial reward, whereas a strategic attack is the coordination of multiple tactical attacks (and on a much larger scale) against multiple target networks for strategic advantage or to preempt an adversary from getting one. The targets of tactical attacks are random and opportunistic, taking advantage of software vulnerabilities and user ignorance, whereas strategic attacks target a higher-level process and are intelligence driven and carefully planned and orchestrated.[11]

For example, strategic attacks may include infiltrating strategic infrastructure, targeting telecommunications infrastructure, and aggregating information in specific technology areas such as stealth technology. The ability to understand strategic attacks requires an understanding of (1) the business functions and processes supported by individual networks; (2) the business relationships between networks; and (3) the sharing of tactical attack data among contractors, suppliers, and target entities. The information gleaned by threats to these business relationships is used to guide and direct strategic attacks.[12,13]

Components of the critical infrastructure include highways, airports and aircraft, trains and railways, bus lines, shipping and boat lines, trucking systems and supply networks for basic goods, and electric power plants and lines, along with oil and gas lines and utilities of all kinds (including water and sewer systems), landlines and cell phone systems, computer networks, television, and radio (not only that which is publicly accessible, but that controlled by private or government entities in special networks or on special frequencies), banks and other financial institutions, and security, fire, hospital, and emergency services. Each element of the critical infrastructure is so vital that if it were removed from the equation, even temporarily, the entire nation would experience monumental repercussions. Even when the infrastructure of a particular area is threatened, the results can be disastrous. This can include telecommunications, energy, banking and finance, transportation, water systems, and emergency services.[14] Of course, strategic targets also include critical elements of the government such as defense, intelligence, and other agencies considered of high value to an adversary.

It is no secret that foreign cyberspace operations against U.S. public- and private-sector systems are increasing in number and sophistication. U.S. government networks are probed millions of times every day, and successful penetrations have led to the loss of thousands of sensitive files from U.S. networks and those of U.S. allies and industry partners. Moreover, this threat continues to evolve as evidence grows of adversaries focusing on the development of increasingly sophisticated and potentially dangerous capabilities.[15]

**Tactical**

Tactical cyber threats are typically surgical by nature, have highly specific targeting, and are technologically sophisticated. Given the specific nature of the attack, the cost of development is typically high. Repeatability is less significant for tactical attacks than for strategic attacks. Tactical attacks can be adjuncts to strategic attacks; in some cases, they serve as a force multiplier or augment other activities such as a military campaign or as a supplementary action to a special-interest action group. Given the surgical nature of these attacks, they are also popular for use in subversive operations. Given the cost of these attacks, they are typically financed by well-funded private entities and governments that are often global in nature and popularity—a country, a business, or a special-interest group.[16]

An example of a tactical cyber attack (which was leveraged for strategic purposes) is the Stuxnet worm. The U.S. and Israeli governments, aiming to subvert nuclear power plants in Iran, likely designed the Stuxnet worm. However, it ended up infecting more than just the intended target, Iran. It impacted a host of countries, including India, the United States, and Great Britain. By September 2010, more than 100,000+ unique hosts had been infected by this worm.[17] Stuxnet was unique in the way it was designed. It propagated through more than one medium (e.g., flash drives and Internet connections). It affected Windows systems and exploited known patched and unknown vulnerabilities in the operating system. However, these Windows systems were not the actual targets of this worm. After infecting a host, it would look for a specific industrial control system, the Programmable Logic Controller made by Siemens®. Apparently, this controller was being used by Iran in its nuclear power plants. If it did not detect the particular controller software, it would not do anything but would wait to propagate around to other hosts. If it did find the controller software, it would infect and change it.[18,19]

**User Specific**

User-targeted specific software attacks can be strategic, tactical, or opportunistic. They may involve an attack targeting a privilege escalation of a specific user that exploits a vulnerability in software to gain access to resources and information that would normally be unrestricted to the user, including data on the specific user machine or resources that the user can access. Strategic attacks are a superset that leverages tactical and/or user-specific attacks.

User-specific cyber threats can be strategic, tactical, or personal in nature, and target personal devices that may be either consumer or enterprise owned. The use of strategic, tactical, or publicly available methods to exploit specific individuals or general populations of users for monetary, political, or personal gain can be specifically targeted to a user as a primary target or as a means to get to another target or the random exploitation of a user as a target of opportunity. In many ways, most strategic and tactical attacks are a form of user attack. The difference between these attacks and user-specific attacks are those of scale. An example of this type of attack is to target a user by installing a keylogger on their system with the intent to use it for immediate financial benefit (e.g., to get passwords to log onto bank accounts), unauthorized access to someone else's email account (for spying on a spouse or celebrities), or to target a quiz with the intention to get around actual results. All these attacks are of benefit to a handful of individuals. Examples of attacks in these categories are ransomware; credit card harvesting; targeting of specific individuals for monetary gains (bank accounts, Social Security numbers, and so on); unauthorized access to social media sites, emails, and other online information with intent to blackmail, exploit, or embarrass individuals; identify theft; phishing attacks; and exploitation of "smart home" products. Readers will be familiar with most of these attacks. Ransomware is a kind of malware that tricks users into believing that there is no way out for them except to pay to get rid of a nuisance. An example of such an attack would be locking a user's desktop and asking for a payment to unlock it. Such attacks were initially found in Russia but have spread to other countries over the last few years.[20]

### 4.3.2.2 Gaining Credentials

Use of credentials is one of the most common aspects of applications. Be it a Web application or a mobile client application, applications often need to interact with services that require authentication. To be able to interact with services successfully, applications must have a way to store and supply credentials.[21] Login credentials are typically passwords or codes of some sort that are typically connected to a user name in the target location to be exploited. There are primarily five ways that attackers steal passwords:

1. **The theft of a database containing your login credentials.** This is one of the largest sources of stolen credentials to date.
2. **Phishing and social engineering attacks.** This is a method in which a hacker will send a phishing email to steal your account information or trick you into clicking a malicious link and entering your credentials on a false site.
3. **Keyloggers, browser injectors, and other malware.** Hackers may try to get users to download malware (a malicious software program) to capture your login credentials, payment information, and other artifacts (including private information).
4. **Password attacks.** Password attacks, like a brute force attack, use automated software programs designed to crack or guess your password.
5. **WiFi monitoring.** Never sign into an account while connected to a public or insecure WiFi connection if you are not protected by software such as a VPN. Hackers can use readily-available network monitoring tools to intercept your credentials and other data.[22,23]

One of the most highly visible examples of an attack that exploited its ability to gain unauthorized access to credentials is the SolarWinds attack. A sophisticated hacking syndicate took advantage of Pulse Secure and a second SolarWinds Orion vulnerability for nearly a year to steal credentials. The advanced persistent threat (APT) group first connected to the unidentified victim's network through a Pulse Secure virtual private network (VPN) appliance starting in March 2020 by masquerading as teleworking employees. From there, the hackers moved laterally to the victim's SolarWinds Orion server, installed Supernova malware, and stole credentials to compromise computers at the National Finance Center. The perpetrators injected Sunburst malware into a SolarWinds Orion update downloaded by nearly 18,000 customers between March 2020 and June 2020. Supernova is placed directly on a system that hosts SolarWinds Orion and is designed to appear as part of the SolarWinds product. The APT group likely exploited an authentication bypass vulnerability in the SolarWinds Orion application programming interface (API) that allows a remote attacker to execute API commands. The hackers then likely leveraged this vulnerability to bypass the authentication to the SolarWinds appliance and then used the Orion API to run commands with the same privileges as the SolarWinds appliance.[24]

### 4.3.2.3 Exploiting Software Flaws

Every sector of the global economy relies on software—from energy to transportation, finance, and banking; telecommunications; public health; emergency services; water; chemical, defense, manufacturing, and food industries; agriculture; right down to the postal and shipping sector. Anything that threatens that software, in effect, poses a threat to our lives. Because of all the potential harm that could occur from exploitation of coding defects, the product not only has to work right (*quality*), it also has to be secure (*security*).

Unfortunately, the following are as true as they were a few years ago. The 2005 U.S. President's Information Technology Advisory Committee (PITAC) report stated: "Commonly used software engineering practices permit dangerous errors, such as improper handling of buffer overflows, which enable hundreds of attack programs to compromise millions of computers every year."[25] This happens mainly because "commercial software engineering today lacks the scientific underpinnings and rigorous controls needed to produce high-quality, secure products at acceptable cost."[26] A U.S. Department of Homeland Security 2006 Draft, "Security in the Software Lifecycle," states the following:

> The most critical difference between secure software and insecure software lies in the nature of the processes and practices used to specify, design, and develop the software

> . . . correcting potential vulnerabilities as early as possible
> in the software development lifecycle, mainly through the
> adoption of security-enhanced process and practices, is far
> more cost-effective than the currently pervasive approach
> of developing and releasing frequent patches to operational
> software.[27]

Software is only as secure as the quality and relevance of
the best practices that the software development team uses.
Software security must be built in from the very beginning of
the development process. It must be a critical part of the design
from the start and included in every subsequent development
phase all the way through fielding a complete system. Correcting
vulnerabilities as early as possible in the software development
life cycle (SDLC) through the adoption of security-enhanced
processes and practices is far more cost effective than attempting to diagnose and correct such problems after the system goes
into production. This will greatly reduce the need to patch the
software to fix security holes discovered by others after release
of the product, which will degrade the reputation and credibility
of the vendor and adversely impact it financially. Today, we are
seeing an increased need for security in software development in
that security requirements, design, and defensive principles have
to be worked into the traditional SDLC and, most important, in
choosing security development practices that embrace this need
throughout all the activities of the SDLC. Although security is
not a natural component of the way industry has been building
software in years past, we believe that security improvements to
development processes are possible, practical, and essential in
the DevOps pipeline. Finally, software executives, leaders, and
managers must support the robust coding practices and required
security enhancements as required by business-relevant security as
well as support the staffing requirements, scheduling, budgeting,
and resource allocations required for this type of work to be
successful in the DevOps environment.

A side effect of the cyber approach is that it has given us the ability to do the above at a scale, distance, and degree of anonymity previously unthought of from jurisdictionally protected locations through remote exploitation and attacks. This gives government, criminal groups, and activists abilities to proxy prime perpetuators to avoid responsibility, detection, and political fallout.

Although there is much publicity regarding network security, the real Achilles' heel is the (insecure) software that provides the potential ability for total control and/or modification of a target as described above. The criticality of software security as we move quickly toward this new age of tasks previously relegated to the human mind being replaced by software-driven machines cannot be underestimated. It is for this reason that we have written this book. In contrast, and for the foreseeable future, software programs are and will be written by humans. This also means that new software will keep building on legacy code or software that was written prior to security being taken seriously, or before sophisticated attacks became prevalent. As long as humans write the programs, the key to successful security for these programs is in making the software development program process more efficient and effective. Although the approach of this book includes people, process, and technology approaches to software security, we believe the people element of software security is still the most important part to manage as long as software is developed, managed, and exploited by humans.

The Gartner Group® reports that more than 70 percent of current business security vulnerabilities are found within software applications rather than the network boundaries.[28] A focus on application security has thus emerged to reduce the risk of poor software development, integration, and deployment. As a result, software assurance quickly became an information assurance (IA) focus area in the financial, government, and manufacturing sectors to reduce the risk of unsecure code: Security built into the software development life cycle (SDLC) makes good business sense.

What is the primary target of hackers, cybercriminals, and nation-state cyber warriors? It is insecure code. What has quickly become the highest unnecessary cost to software development? It is flaws arising from insecure code in software products that have already been released to the market. When these flaws are discovered and/or exploited, they cause interruptions in current product development cycles to fix something that should have been fixed during the development of the product that has the flaw; they cause delays in product release dates because individuals or teams working on current products are pulled off cycle to fix issues in a previously released product; and they result in vulnerability scope creep because vulnerabilities discovered in one product may affect the security of others in Web, Software as a Service (SaaS), and cloud applications. They also create legal issues, reputation degradation, and public relations nightmares, such as those experienced by Sony®, Symantec®, and RSA® over the years. They can also result in significant liability to the company. In an age of extensive regulations governing privacy and exposure of data, this quickly adds up even for big corporations. The point here is that even as the high-tech world, its consumers, customers, regulators, and the media have started to realize that not only is it imperative to fix software security problems, there is, in fact, a way to solve these issues in the form of a structured security software.

The cost associated with addressing software problems increases as the lifecycle of a project matures. The cost of finding and fixing a bug after a software product has been released can be 100 times more expensive than solving the problem in the requirements or design called the security development lifecycle (SDL). The SDL has as its base components all of the activities and security controls needed to develop industry- and government-compliant and best practices–hardened software. A knowledgeable staff as well as secure software policies and controls are required in order to truly prevent, identify, and mitigate exploitable vulnerabilities within developed systems. Patching vulnerable software after release can be a costly way of securing applications. Furthermore, patches are not always applied by owners/users of the vulnerable software; patches can also contain more vulnerabilities. Developers must take the time to code cleanly and eradicate every possible security flaw before the code goes into production.

### 4.3.2.4 Malicious Coders

Malicious coders refer to viruses, worms, Trojan horses, logic bombs, and other "uninvited" software. Although it is sometimes mistakenly associated only with personal computers, such types of malicious code can attack other platforms. The actual costs that have been attributed to the presence of malicious code most often include the cost of system outages and the cost of staff time for those who are involved in finding the *malware* and repairing the systems. Frequently, these costs are quite significant.

Today, we are subject to a vast number of virus incidents. This fact has generated much discussion on the issues of organizational liability and must be considered. Viruses are the most common case of malicious code. In today's modern computing platforms, some form of antivirus software must be included in order to cope with this threat. To do otherwise can be extremely costly.

### 4.3.2.5 Exploiting Humans through Social Engineering

No matter how strong an organization's security is, the attacker will always seek out and find the path of least resistance. However, when your defensive security posture is strong, the weakest leak is often the employee of the company being targeted. Data breaches can be a result of employee error or an inside job. With the typical focus on technical defenses, employees are often overlooked.

Cybersecurity measures are frequently focused on threats from outside an organization rather than threats posed by untrustworthy individuals inside an organization. However, insider threats are the source of many losses in critical infrastructure industries.

Additionally, well-publicized insiders have caused irreparable harm to national security interests. An insider threat is defined as the threat that an employee or a contractor will use his or her authorized access, wittingly or unwittingly, to do harm to the security of the United States. Although policy violations can be the result of carelessness or accident, the primary focus of this project is preventing deliberate and intended actions, such as malicious exploitation, theft, or destruction of data or the compromise of networks, communications, or other information technology (IT) resources.

In today's digital workplace, companies don't only have to protect themselves from outside hackers—they also have to develop a process to guard against insider threats. These threats can include the poor cyber hygiene habits of employees as well as malicious actions such as fraud, theft of intellectual property or confidential information, and even intentional damage to computer systems.

Additionally, the insider threat threshold is wide. Even well-intentioned team members can misplace equipment, use inadequate passwords, or fall prey to a phishing scheme. Further, malicious attacks can come from anyone who has inside information about your company's systems and vulnerabilities. That can include everyone from unhappy or unscrupulous current employees to past employees, vendors, and contractors.

The weakest link in security will always be people, and the easiest way to break into a system is to engineer your way in through the human interface. Most every hacker group has engaged in some form of social engineering, in combination with other activities, over the years, and they have been able to break into many corporations as a result. In this type of attack, the attacker chooses a mark, whom they can scam to gain a password, user ID, or other usable information. Because most administrators and employees of companies are concerned with providing efficiency and helping users, they may be unaware that the person they are speaking to is not a legitimate user. And because there are no formal procedures for establishing whether an end user is legitimate, the attacker often gains a tremendous amount of information in a very short amount of time, often with no way to trace the information leak back to the attackers.

Social engineering begins with the goal of obtaining information about a person or business and can range in activities from dumpster diving to cold calls or impersonations. As acknowledged in the movies, many hackers and criminals have realized that a wealth of valuable information is often laying in trash bins, waiting to be emptied by a disposal company. Most corporations do not adequately dispose of information, and trash bins often contain information that may identify employees or customers. This information is not secured and is available to anyone willing to dive into the dumpster at night and look for it—hence, the term "dumpster diving."

Other information is readily available via deception. Most corporations do not contain security measures that adequately address deception. What happens when the protocol is followed properly, but the person being admitted is not whom they say they are? Many groups utilize members of their group in a fashion that would violate protocols so as to gather information about what a corporation's admittance policy is. Often the multi-person attack will result in gaining admittance to the company and, ultimately, the information desired. Using the bathroom or going for a drink of water is always a great excuse for exiting from a meeting, often one during which you will not have an escort. Most corporations do not have terminal locking policies, and this is another way an attacker can gain access or load software that could pierce the company's firewall. So long as the person entering the corporation looks the part and can act according to the role the company has defined for access, it is unlikely that person will be detected.

Remotely, social engineering actually becomes less challenging. There are no visual expectations to meet, and people are very willing to participate with a little coaxing. As is often the case, giving away something free can always be a method for entry.

Many social engineering situations involve sending along a piece of software or something of value for free. Embedded within the free software, Trojans, viruses, and worms can go undetected, bypassing system and network security. Since most security that protects the local machine has a hard time differentiating between real and fake software, it is often not risky for the attacker to deliver a keylogger or Trojan to the victim machine. Equally effective, the customer support or employee support personnel can be duped into aiding a needy user with their passwords and with access to information they do not necessarily know about.

In today's environment, anybody can be fooled. Everybody, including executives, can be spoofed with the advent of social media, providing significant details about your personal life.

### 4.3.2.6 Exploiting Business Partners

You are only as strong as your weakest link. To be competitive, most companies want to develop new products to improve their competitiveness and profitability, and to access new markets, and they will seek alternatives such as a partnerships or mergers and acquisitions (M&As) when they cannot do this with their current resources. If the business partner has less-secure security practices than your organization, you will have an increased risk posture. This is a very common concern for security teams from the acquired company that are involved in a M&A. Think of all the critical information housed at your accounting firm, your tax firm, and your external legal counsel.

This issue is important and much more complex when dealing with supply chains. As organizations connect, demand, and design supply chains, they create multi-organizational dependencies. Even the biggest companies with teams of professionals face risks. Especially vulnerable are smaller manufacturers without a dedicated cybersecurity team. Even when a business is proactive about cybersecurity, its supply chain may not be. Since the strongest chain must rely on its weakest link, business leaders owe it to themselves to learn the basics of cybersecurity to include trusted security advisors. An organization may not be able to stop every threat, but it can surely do more to ensure that its weakest link is not ignorance or weak policies. The well-known Target® credit card data breech of 2013 was launched by compromising permissioned credentials of a third-party HVAC technician, which were used to traverse the network and gain access to the credit card information.

### 4.3.2.7 Ransomware

Ransomware is a type of malware from cryptovirology that threatens to publish the victim's personal data or perpetually block access to it unless a ransom is paid. Although some simple ransomware may lock the system so that it is not difficult for a knowledgeable person to reverse it, more advanced malware uses a technique called cryptoviral extortion. It encrypts the victim's files, making them inaccessible, and demands a ransom payment to decrypt them.[29–32] In a properly implemented cryptoviral extortion attack, recovering the files without the decryption key is an intractable problem—and difficult-to-trace digital currencies such as paysafecard or Bitcoin and other cryptocurrencies are used for the ransoms, making tracing and prosecuting the perpetrators difficult. Ransomware attacks are typically carried out using a Trojan disguised as a legitimate file that the user is tricked into downloading or opening when it arrives as an email attachment. However, one high-profile example, the WannaCry worm, traveled automatically between computers without user interaction.[33,34]

Unfortunately, in many cases, once the ransomware has been released into your device, there is little you can do unless you have a backup or security software in place. Nevertheless, it is sometimes possible to help infected users to regain access to their encrypted files or locked systems, without having to pay. Websites such as https://www.nomoreransom.org/ have created a repository of keys and applications that can decrypt data locked by different types of ransomware and provide other support. Prevention is possible. Following simple cybersecurity advice can help you to avoid becoming a victim of ransomware.

A ransomware attack is typically delivered via an email attachment that could be an executable file, an archive, or an image. Once the attachment is opened, the malware is released into the user's system. Cybercriminals can also plant the malware on websites. When a user visits the site unknowingly, the malware is released into the system.

The infection is not immediately apparent to the user. The malware operates silently in the background until the system or data-locking mechanism is deployed. Then a dialogue box appears that tells the user the data has been locked and demands a ransom to unlock it again. By then, it is too late to save the data through any security measures. Any consumer and any business can be a victim of ransomware. Cybercriminals are not selective and are often looking to hit as many users as possible in order to obtain the highest profit.

Ransomware attacks against businesses are growing because cybercriminals know that organizations are more likely to pay as the data held captive is typically both sensitive and vital for business continuity. In addition, it can sometimes be more expensive to restore backups than to pay a ransom. Ransomware continues to be on a steep rise. From 2015 to 2020, there were more than 1,040 families of this malware identified,[35] and it evolved quickly. With each new variant comes better encryption and new features. This is not something you can ignore!

One of the reasons why it is so difficult to find a single solution is because encryption in itself is not malicious. It is actually a good development, and many benign programs use it.

The first crypto malware used a symmetric-key algorithm, with the same key for encryption and decryption. Corrupted information could usually be deciphered successfully with the assistance of security companies. Over time, cybercriminals began to implement asymmetric cryptography algorithms that use two separate keys—a public one to encrypt files and a private one, which is needed for decryption.

The CryptoLocker Trojan is one of the most famous pieces of ransomware. It also uses a public-key algorithm. As each computer is infected, it connects to the command-and-control server to download the public key. The private key is accessible only to the criminals who wrote the CryptoLocker software. Usually, the victim has no more than 72 hours to pay the ransom before their private key is deleted forever, and it is impossible to decrypt any files without this key.

You have to think about prevention first. Most antivirus software already includes a component that helps to identify a ransomware threat in the early stages of infection, without occurring the loss of any sensitive data. It is important for users to ensure that this functionality is switched on in their antivirus solution.

In mid-summer of 2021, hackers behind a mass ransomware attack exploited multiple previously unknown vulnerabilities in IT management software made by Kaseya Ltd. More than 70 managed service providers were impacted, resulting in more than 350 further impacted organizations, and victims in 17 countries have been identified. It should be noted how ingenious the supply-chain ransomware attacks were from a criminal standpoint. The attackers not only encrypted the systems, but they also took the recovery tool out of the equation.[36]

Some eye-opening statistics for ransomware include the following:

- The first documented ransomware attack happened in 1989 and targeted the healthcare industry.
- Launched in 2017, WannaCry is considered the biggest and most widespread ransomware attack in history. It's estimated to have crippled 200,000 computers in 150 countries, putting the world in a state of frenzy for four days.
- In 2021, ransomware attacks against businesses occurred every 11 seconds.

- On average, organizations pay a ransom of $233,217.00.
- The global cost associated with ransomware recovery exceeded $20 billion in 2021.
- Ransomware perpetrators carry out more than 4,000 attacks daily.[37]

### 4.3.2.8 Advanced Persistent Threats (APTs)

An APT is a stealthy threat actor, typically a nation-state or state-sponsored group that gains unauthorized access to a computer network and remains undetected for an extended period.[38,39] In recent times, the term may also refer to non–state-sponsored groups conducting large-scale targeted intrusions for specific goals.[40]

Such threat actors' motivations are typically political or economic. Every major business sector has recorded instances of cyberattacks by advanced actors with specific goals—whether to steal, spy, or disrupt. These targeted sectors include the government, defense, financial services, legal services, the manufacturing industry, telecoms, consumer goods, and many more.[41-43] Some groups utilize traditional espionage vectors, including social engineering, human intelligence, and infiltration to gain access to a physical location to enable network attacks. The purpose of these attacks is to install custom malware (malicious software).[44]

The median "dwell-time," the time an APT attack goes undetected, differs widely between regions. FireEye reported the mean dwell-time for 2018 in the Americas as 71 days, EMEA as 177 days, and APAC as 204 days.[45] Such a long dwell-time allows attackers a significant amount of time to go through the attack cycle, propagate, and achieve their objective.[46]

Cozy Bear, classified by the U.S. federal government as advanced persistent threat APT29, is a Russian hacker group believed to be associated with one or more intelligence agencies of Russia.[47] As of July 2021, Cozy Bear was implicated in a number of high-profile attacks and was likely the most well-known APT to the general public. APT29 has used social media sites such as Twitter® or

GitHub®, as well as cloud storage services, to relay commands and extract data from compromised networks. The group relays commands via images containing hidden and encrypted data. Information is extracted from a compromised network, and files are uploaded to cloud storage services.[48]

Another alert by the U.S. government in July 2021 was issued over what it describes as brute-force password attacks that are being launched from a specially crafted Kubernetes cluster. The attacks have been attributed to a unit within Russia's foreign intelligence agency, the General Staff Main Intelligence Directorate (GRU); the NSA said it's the same GRU unit that has been identified as the APT28 or Fancy Bear threat group. The stolen accounts are used to log into the targeted company's network, where the attackers then look to exploit elevation of privilege and remote code execution vulnerabilities to obtain administrator rights; these vulnerabilities include two Microsoft Exchange Server® laws, CVE 2020-0688 and CVE 2020-17144. From there, the hackers look to move laterally through the network, eventually arriving at a mail server or other valuable data cache. Once the data and account details have been collected and uploaded to another server, the attackers install web shells and administrator accounts, giving them persistence on the network and the ability to get back in at a later date.[49]

### 4.3.2.9 Infrastructure Attacks

Devastating results can occur from the loss of supporting infra-structure. This infrastructure loss can include power failures (outages, spikes, and brownouts), loss of communications, water outages and leaks, sewer problems, lack of infrastructure services, fires, floods, civil unrest, and strikes. A loss of infrastructure often results in system downtime, sometimes in the most unexpected ways. Countermeasures against loss of physical and infrastructure support include the addition of redundant systems and the estab-lishment of recurring backup processes. Because of the damage these types of threats can cause, the Critical Infrastructure Act was enacted.

### 4.3.2.10 Industrial Espionage

A company might be subject to industrial espionage simply because its competitors share some level of sensitive customer information that might be worth millions for interested parties, which range from governments to the press to corporate and private entities. This situation might be encouraging enough for many hackers to tempt fate and attempt to obtain such information. There could be active attempts to retrieve information without authority by hacking, sniffing, and other measures. A case of espionage can have serious consequences for a company, in terms of incurring the cost of lawsuits and resulting damage awards. This situation can also can also devastate a company's reputation in the marketplace.

Formally defined, industrial espionage is the act of gathering proprietary data from private companies or governments for the purpose of aiding others. Industrial espionage can be perpetrated either by companies seeking to improve their competitive advantage or by governments seeking to aid their domestic industries. Foreign industrial espionage carried out by a government is often referred to as economic espionage. Since information is processed and stored on computer systems, computer security can help protect against such threats; it can do little, however, to reduce the threat of authorized employees selling that information. Three particularly damaging main targets of stolen information are pricing information, manufacturing process information, and product development and specification information. Other types of information stolen includes customer lists, research, sales data, personal data, compensation data, cost data, proposals, and strategic goals.

Within the area of economic espionage, the Central Intelligence Agency (CIA) has stated that its main objective is obtaining information related to technology, but that information on U.S. government policy deliberation concerning foreign affairs and information on commodities, interest rates, and other economic factors is also a target. The Federal Bureau of Investigation (FBI) concurs that technology-related information is the main target but also lists corporate proprietary information, such as negotiating positions and other contracting data, as a target.

### 4.3.2.11 Cyber War

Cyberwarfare has been defined by government security expert Richard A. Clarke, in his book *Cyber War* (May 2010), as "actions by a nation-state to penetrate another nation's computers or networks for the purposes of causing damage or disruption."[50] *The Economist* describes cyberwarfare as "the fifth domain of warfare."[51]

From some of the quotes above, you can see that there is an acceptance that when we are speaking in terms of war, cyber and physical are not separate from each other, they are merely different theaters of war. Like other theaters of war, they all have commonalities but typically have different weapons, tactics, and command structures; different rules of engagement; different forms of targets and different methods to identify a target; different expectations of collateral damage; and different expectations of risk. Cyber attacks can have a great impact, but not necessarily focused or highly targeted, such as disrupting communications, affecting the processing of information, and disrupting portions of systems that inhibit normal functions.

In contrast to this, when the government or military use the term cyber war, they are typically thinking of highly targeted and impactful eventualities, such as shutting down power, phones, air traffic control, trains, and emergency services. Cyber attacks are not limited to cyberspace; there is both intended and unintended collateral damage outside the realm of cyber. For example, manipulating a SCADA control system in a chemical plant or critical infrastructure facility may cause an intended or unintended explosion, possible area contamination, or a toxic chemical spill or floating toxic cloud.

It is no secret that foreign cyberspace operations against U.S. public and private sector systems are increasing in number and sophistication. U.S. government networks are probed millions of times every day, and successful penetrations have led to the loss of thousands of sensitive files from U.S. networks and those of U.S. allies and industry partners. Moreover, this threat continues to evolve as evidence grows of adversaries focusing on the development of increasingly sophisticated and potentially dangerous capabilities.[52]

The potential for small groups to have an asymmetric impact in cyberspace creates very real incentives for malicious activity. Beyond formal governmental activities, cybercriminals can control botnets with millions of infected hosts. The tools and techniques developed by cybercriminals are increasing in sophistication at an incredible rate, and many of these capabilities can be purchased cheaply on the Internet. Whether the goal is monetary, access to intellectual property, or the disruption of critical systems, the rapidly evolving threat landscape presents a complex and vital challenge for national and economic security.

Because much of our nation's critical infrastructure depends on computing technology, it is more than just a little significant that adversarial countries are probing and penetrating our networks on a daily basis. Adversaries continue to work 24×7 to constantly probe and penetrate defenses until they find a way in. Even though defense and other government organizations have built teams to protect their digital infrastructures with defenses in place, breaches still occur because vulnerabilities still exist.

The cyber world is difficult to envision because of its virtual nature and scope. It is not entirely virtual, however. It is integrated with the physical world through data centers, servers, routers, switches, cables, modems, communication towers, PCs, mobile devices, keyboards, printers, and storage devices.

Even though cyber is virtualized and distributed, its physical interconnection with communication and data distribution systems can be greatly impacted by disrupting cyber assets that may or may not be within the borders of that country, such as satellites, switches in bordering countries, provider networks, and myriad other computer services. This can also be true for systems such as those used for power distribution, water services, or emergency services. A cyber weapon could be constructed that renders military aircraft ineffective or disrupts targeting on navigation systems of tanks or ground-to-air missile systems. In fact, electronic warfare systems have done this for decades. Methodology and potential anonymity of an attack of this nature are a few of the differences that distinguish how a cyber attack impacts a cyber asset and how it will materialize in some manner directly or indirectly in the physical world. Cyberwarfare is a theater of war, and it will be shared with other theaters of war in the physical domain in future conflicts.

Cyber is virtual, ubiquitous, and interconnected. It's more than just the Internet and the cloud. It is a complex network of digital systems interacting with other systems and transporting information that plays an increasingly critical role in how humans live, survive, and function. Due to its criticality, cyber has high value and is integral to our survival. Because it can be destroyed, it means there are corresponding weapons and methodologies to deliver that destruction. This methodology and its associated weaponry is cyberwarfare, and the best defense against it is a good defense.

It is no secret that foreign cyberspace operations against U.S. public and private sector systems are increasing in number and sophistication. U.S. government networks are probed millions of times every day and successful penetrations have led to the loss of thousands of sensitive files from U.S. networks and those of U.S. allies and industry partners. Moreover, this threat continues to evolve as evidence grows of adversaries focusing on the development of increasingly sophisticated and potentially dangerous capabilities.[53]

### 4.3.2.12 Reactive versus Proactive Organizations

A proactive approach to cybersecurity includes preemptively identifying security weaknesses and adding processes to identify threats before they occur. On the other hand, a reactive approach involves responding to incidents such as hacks and data breaches after they occur and have already made their way into your network. In contrast to reactive security, proactive security methods are more concerned with indicators of attack (IoA) and actually take charge of all processes, technology, systems, and people, with the goal of preparing for an attack, not waiting for it to happen.[54,55] There are other benefits of a proactive cybersecurity strategy. They include the following:

- Your team isn't constantly reacting.
- Actively prevent breaches.
- Catch up with the bad guys.
- Sniff out an inside job.
- Find mistakes.
- Improve compliance.
- Proactivity really works.[56]

It has almost become cliché to say that an organization must develop a proactive security posture, but this critically important strategy is still a relatively new concept for many. Even after accepting that they must move to more "proactive" security, many organizations still have problems in understanding how do to so in a manner that will have the greatest impact on reducing their risk. This disconnect may lie in people's misperceptions of what it means to truly be "proactive."

Several years ago, intrusion detection and prevention activities became the norm at any organization serious about cybersecurity. As soon as people realized that these assessments were being implemented too few and far between, security leaders began to use continuous or "real-time" monitoring of network vulnerabilities to get a better handle on threats like "Zero Day" exploits and to reduce the amount of time it takes to respond to attacks—a move some called proactive.

Although there have been steps in the right direction, the entire strategy still remains focused on reacting. To truly be proactive, security leaders need to engage in advanced penetration testing, simulations, and real-time vulnerability testing to attempt to hack into their own networks (even at the code level) in order to understand where the true vulnerabilities lie and what needs to be done to fix them.

A true shift to proactive security means looking at new technologies and methodologies versus simply increasing the frequency in which we use the same technologies and techniques. One theory as to why this shift has not already occurred involves the ego of the chief information officer (CIO), who is hesitant to attack a network they built and point out its vulnerabilities. This requires cultural change, where leaders are not worried about looking bad and failing at complying, but rather are confident that they will be rewarded based on the performance of their actions.

### 4.3.3 Compromise Impacts

Impacts from security compromises are typically very serious and, in some cases, put a company out of business. In this section, we will cover some of the biggest and most detrimental consequences of having their business information compromised, including business disruption, loss of assets, loss of intellectual property, loss of customer personally identifiable information (PII), economic damage, and reputations/market cap.

#### 4.3.3.1 Business Disruption

Business disruption has become a main attack objective for more adversaries. According to a report by U.S.-based cybersecurity firm CrowdStrike, 36 percent of all incidents it investigated in 2019 had business disruption as their main objective. These attacks were largely caused by ransomware, destructive malware, or DoS attacks. Although business disruption came right on top when it comes to attack impacts, data theft followed right behind. It was observed in 25 percent of all breaches the company investigated. Data theft includes the theft of intellectual property (IP), personally identifiable information (PII), and personal health information (PHI).[57,58]

### 4.3.3.2 Loss of Assets

When key business assets are not adequately protected from cybersecurity breaches, organizations can experience dire consequences. To implement a security program, you must first identify the assets you are trying to protect, the threats against those assets, and how vulnerable those assets are to the various threats.

Business assets can be categorized in a number of ways. One of the simpler descriptions is that described by the 2005 revision of ISO/IEC 27001, which defines an asset as "anything that has value to the organization."[59] Since ISO 27001 focuses on preservation of confidentiality, integrity, and availability of information, this means that assets can be:

- Hardware—for example, laptops, servers, printers, as well as mobile phones or USB memory sticks.
- Software—not only the purchased software, but also freeware.
- Information—not only in electronic media (databases, files in PDF, Word, Excel, and other formats), but also in paper and other forms.
- Infrastructure—for example, offices, electricity, air conditioning—because a compromise of those assets can cause lack of availability of information.
- People—also considered assets because they have lots of information in their heads, which is very often not available in other forms.

- Outsourced services—for example, legal services or cleaning services, as well as online services such as Dropbox® or Gmail™. It is true that these are not assets in the pure sense of the word, but such services need to be controlled very similarly to assets, so they are very often included in asset management.[60]

### 4.3.3.3 Loss of Intellectual Property

Loss of IP is an intangible cost associated with loss of exclusive control over trade secrets, copyrights, investment plans, and other proprietary and confidential information that can lead to loss of competitive advantage, loss of revenue, and lasting and potentially irreparable economic damage to the company. Types of IP include, but are not limited to, patents, designs, copyrights, trademarks, and trade secrets. Unlike other types of IP, trade secrets are protected indefinitely until publicly disclosed. Similar to the value of a trade name, the value of IP is estimated by approximating how much another party would pay to license that IP.[61,62]

These kinds of scenarios keep executives up at night for good reason: IP is the heart of the 21st-century company, an essential motor driving innovation, competitiveness, and the growth of businesses and the economy as a whole. IP can constitute more than 80 percent of a single company's value today. Though IP theft is hardly new, and some IP may still be attainable only through physical means, the digital world has made theft easier.[63] It's no surprise, then, that criminals find this to be an attractive target.

Cybercrime is big business. IP and intangible assets may make up more than 85 percent of a company's value today. Recovering from an IP breach can be impossible. Once data is stolen, it is impossible to control who accesses, trades, sells, and benefits from it. And until organizations make the decision to invest in their own cybersecurity on an ongoing basis, they will continue to incur damage.[64]

### 4.3.3.4 Loss of Customer Personally Identifiable Information

When personal data has been exposed or stolen, customers feel betrayed. Company privacy policies may not be read, but customers believe that any company that collects their personal data has a responsibility to protect it. A data breach is seen as a breach of the company's responsibility to keep personal data private and secure, and many customers will take their business elsewhere after such a privacy violation.

Several regulations have been put in place to ensure the protection of sensitive PII by the organizations that collect them. This is due to the impact of the theft of such information. The demand for PII is on the rise on the dark Web due to the value it provides to criminal elements. Once a criminal has possession of personal details, such as name, date of birth, real physical address, and current contact details, it's very easy for a skilled social engineer to scam a target. This is one of the reasons why governments have ensured that there are very tough laws to protect PII.[65]

### 4.3.3.5 Economic Damage

As of 2018, cybercrime had already become an economic disaster in many countries. It is estimated that at least $600,000,000,000 was being drained annually from the global economy through cybercrime. This is quite a huge figure, and its impact is already being felt. The loss of this has affected many factors, including jobs. Cybercrime is hurting the economy and, in turn, hurting the job market.[66]

In the United States, it's estimated that cybercrime has already caused the loss of over 200,000 jobs. The loss of jobs and the drainage of money from a country's economy has made cybercrime a major concern globally. It has been reported that many industries have already had their business secrets stolen. In the United States, it's estimated that a large number of organizations are among those that are not aware of having been breached and their business secrets stolen, which means that the economic loss will likely continue for a while.[67]

In a recent report,[68] Deloitte™ identified 14 business impacts of a cyber incident as they play out over a five-year incident response process—seven direct and seven hidden costs. For the intangible costs, various financial modeling techniques were used to estimate the damage. And the research showed that the direct costs commonly associated with data breaches were far less significant than the "hidden" costs. In Deloitte's scenarios, they accounted for less than 5 percent of the total business impact. Given that impact, chief financial officers (CFOs) should be aware of the following seven hidden costs. The 14 business impacts identified by Deloitte are listed below[69,70]:

**Direct Costs (above the surface)**

- Post-breach customer protection
- Cybersecurity improvements
- Customer breach notification
- Attorney fees and litigation
- Regulatory compliance (HIPAA fines)
- Public relations
- Technical investigation

**Hidden Costs (below the surface)**

- Insurance premium increases
- Increased cost to raise debt
- Operational disruption or destruction
- Lost value of customer relationships
- Value of lost contract revenue
- Devaluation of trade name
- Loss of IP

### 4.3.3.6 Reputations/Market Cap

Reputational loss threatens the public's view of a company or organization. Loss of reputation directly impacts finances for businesses and nonprofits. A loss that causes reputational damage is considered reputational risk. Of course, the loss of reputation will likely have a direct effect on drops in market cap. Corporate consulting experts caution organizations to consider that managing reputational risk is a two-way relationship. Security impacts reputation, and reputation impacts security.

Deloitte, a corporate audit, consulting, advisory, and tax organization, cites that "security risks, including both physical and cyber breaches," caused reputational risks more frequently than other types of risks, according to their 2018 CEO and Board Risk Management survey,[71] Aon™ notes that risk management teams would be wise to avoid taking a simplified approach to risk management. To look at the reverse effects of reputation, Aon recommends that organizations look at the four P's within their companies—products, policies, people, and politics.[72]

Reputational risk can pose a danger to the survival of the largest and best-run businesses by wiping out millions or billions of dollars in market capitalization or future profits.

Cyber risk is any risk from the digital world, including damage to the reputation of a company, such as financial loss, operational disruption, data breaches, and a negative event affecting the information system.[73]

Reputation loss after a cyber attack can have a major impact on businesses. Whereas large companies may be able to absorb the loss of customers that results, for small to medium businesses, reputation damage and loss of customers can prove devastating.

Reputation also relates to trust, and regaining the trust of customers can be much harder to recover from. Once trust in a brand is lost, some customers will leave and never return. Reputation loss after a cyber attack may also result in a difficulty in finding new customers. A few years ago, Radware® conducted a survey to investigate the cost of cyber attacks on businesses. The study revealed that 43 percent of companies that took part in the study said they had experienced negative customer experiences and reputation loss as a result of a successful cyber attack. Previous studies suggest that as many as one third of customers will stop doing business with a company that has experienced a data breach. A study by Gemalto™ paints an even bleaker picture. In a global survey of 10,000 individuals, 70 percent claimed they would stop doing business with a company that had experienced a data breach.[74]

Many organizations spend a lot of money on building their brand in order to keep a certain market share and also to keep investors satisfied. Cyber attacks typically attract negative press, which can lead to damaging a company's brand and reputation. There are many companies that will not survive or will just diminish in influence and market share as a result of losing their trusted brand name. In turn, a significant number of investors will likely start selling their shares to mitigate further losses due to a dropping share price, as customers will always want to buy from companies that they trust. Others of those that hang onto the stock will become bitter "bag holders" in a stock not likely to recover. In many cases, customers will also stop trusting the victim company's goods and services. As we have seen over the last few years, competitors will likely take advantage of the situation and intensify marketing in order to win over the customers and investors of the target company. In short, the impact as a result of damage to the reputation and market cap of a company can be very costly as a result of a compromise.[75]

## 4.4 CHAPTER SUMMARY

If you finished this chapter, you should rightly be concerned about your organization's ability to protect critical assets and rapidly discover when those assets are under attack or have been compromised. Cyber threats derive from infrastructure, system, and software flaws and vulnerabilities, which are weaknesses that can be exploited by cyber attacks or exploitation. These attacks typically fall into two categories: strategic and tactical. Strategic attacks are typically planned and controlled to target information assets, including specifications, technologies, plans, capabilities, procedures, and guidelines, to gain strategic advantage. They are typically conducted by state sponsors (or by entities supported by states), organized crime, or competitors. Tactical attacks are typically random and opportunistic; they target information assets for prestige or financial reward through the use of malware, exploits, hackers, surrogates, insider threat, and chat rooms, and they are conducted by professional hackers, script kiddies, and insiders. In this chapter, we have provided a high-level overview of these type of attacks and exploitation as well as the potential consequences of each. Knowledge of the threat actors and their attack and exploitation methodologies is key to understanding the cybersecurity risk in your organization and has been provided as an example of what your security and/or risk officer should be telling you. Specifically, your organization should have an inventory of key assets mapped to likely adversaries in order to know how to best monitor and protect those assets. Most importantly, this is a key part of the CYBERPHOS cybertax assessment that we describe elsewhere in the book.

## REFERENCES

1. U.S. Department of Defense. (2011, July). Department of Defense Strategy for Operating in Cyberspace. Retrieved from https://csrc .nist.gov/CSRC/media/Projects/ISPAB/documents/DOD-Strategy -for-Operating-in-Cyberspace.pdf
2. Interpol. (2013). Cybercrime. Retrieved from http://www.interpol .int/Crime-areas/Cybercrime/Cybercrime
3. Williams, P. (2013). Organized Crime and Cybercrime: Synergies, Trends, and Responses. Retrieved from http://www.crime-research .org/library/Cybercrime.htm

4. Ibid.
5. Samani, R. and Paget, F. (2011). Cybercrime Exposed—Cybercrime-as-a-Service. McAfee—An Intel Company White Paper. Retrieved from http://www.mcafee.com/us/resources/white-papers/wp-cyber crime-exposed.pdf
6. Ransome, J. and Misra, A. (2014). *Core Software Security: Security at the Source.* Boca Raton (FL): CRC Press/Taylor & Francis Group.
7. Security Alliance—John. (2017, March 3). The Corporation as a Threat Actor. Blog. Retrieved from https://www.secalliance.com /blog/corporation-threat-actor
8. U.S. Department of Justice, Press Release. (2002, February 26). Former Computer Network Administrator at New Jersey High-Tech Form Sentenced to 41 months for Unleashing $10 Million Computer "Time Bomb." Retrieved from https://www.justice.gov /archive/criminal/cybercrime/press-releases/2002/lloydSent.htm
9. Soare, B. (2020, April 30). What Are the Main Vectors of Attack in Cybersecurity and How Do They Work? And How to Protect Your Business from Different Attack Vectors. Blog. Retrieved from https://heimdalsecurity.com/blog/vectors-of-attack/
10. Ransome, J. and Misra, A. (2014). *Core Software Security: Security at the Source* (pp. 328–329). Boca Raton (FL): CRC Press/Taylor & Francis Group.
11. Ransome, J. and Misra, A. (2014). *Core Software Security: Security at the Source* (pp. 327–328). Boca Raton (FL): CRC Press/Taylor & Francis Group.
12. Gilbert, L., Morgan, R., and Keen, A. (2009, May 5). Tactical and Strategic Attack Detection and Prediction. U.S. Patent 7530105. Retrieved from http://www.freepatentsonline.com/7530105.html
13. Ransome, J. and Misra, A. (2014). *Core Software Security: Security at the Source* (p. 328). Boca Raton (FL): CRC Press/Taylor & Francis Group.
14. Gilbert, L., Morgan, R., and Keen, A. (2009, May 5). Tactical and Strategic Attack Detection and Prediction. U.S. Patent 7530105. Retrieved from http://www.freepatentsonline.com/7530105.html
15. U.S. Department of Defense (2011, July). U.S. Department of Defense Strategy for Operating in Cyberspace, p. 3. Retrieved from https://csrc.nist.gov/CSRC/media/Projects/ISPAB/documents /DOD-Strategy-for-Operating-in-Cyberspace.pdf

16. Ransome, J. and Misra, A. (2014). *Core Software Security: Security at the Source* (p. 338). Boca Raton (FL): CRC Press/Taylor & Francis Group.

17. Falliere, N., Murchu, L., and Chien, E. (2011, February). W32. Stuxnet Dossier, Version 1.4—Symantec Security Response. Retrieved from http://www.symantec.com/content/en/us/enterprise/media /security_response/whitepapers/w32_stuxnet_dossier.pdf

18. Schneier, B. (2010, October 7). Stuxnet. Schneier on Security—A Blog Covering Security and Security Technology. Retrieved from https://www.schneier.com/blog/archives/2010/10/stuxnet.html

19. Ransome, J. and Misra, A. (2014). *Core Software Security: Security at the Source* (p. 338). Boca Raton (FL): CRC Press/Taylor & Francis Group.

20. Dunn, J. (2012, March 9). Ransom Trojans Spreading Beyond Russian Heartland: Security Companies Starting to See More Infections. *Techworld*. Retrieved from http://news.techworld.com/security/3343528 /ransom-trojans-spreading-beyond-russian-heartland

21. Srinvas. (2020, November 17). How Are Credentials Used in Applications? Retrieved from https://resources.infosecinstitute. com/topic/how-are-credentials-used-in-applications/

22. Dashlame. (2020, September 8). What Is Credential Stuffing? Blog. Retrieved from https://blog.dashlane.com/hackers-steal -your-reused-passwords-using-credential-stuffing/

23. Pegasus Technologies. (2016, August 31). 5 Most Common Ways Hackers Steal Login Credentials. Retrieved from https://www.pegasus technologies.com/5-most-common-ways-hackers-steal-login-creden tials/

24. Novison, M. (2021, April 22). Hackers Exploit SolarWinds, Pulse Secure for Credential Theft: Feds. Retrieved from https://www .crn.com/news/security/hackers-exploit-solarwinds-pulse-secure-for -credential-theft-feds

25. President's Information Technology Advisory Committee. (2005). Cybersecurity: A Crisis of Prioritization, Executive Office of the President, National Coordination Office for Information Technology Research and Development, 2005, p. 39. Retrieved from http://www .nitrd.gov/Pitac/reports/20050301_cybersecurity/cybersecurity.pdf

26. Ibid.

27. U.S. Department of Homeland Security. (2006). Security in the Software Lifecycle: Making Software Development Processes—and Software Produced by Them—More Secure, DRAFT Version 1.2, p. 13. Retrieved from http://www.cert.org/books/secureswe /SecuritySL.pdf

28. Aras, O., Ciaramitaro, B., and Livermore, J. (2008). Secure Software Development—The Role of IT Audit. *ISACA Journal*, 4. Retrieved from http://www.isaca.org/Journal/Past-Issues/2008/Volume-4 /Pages/Secure-Software-Development-The-Role-of-IT-Audit1.aspx

29. Young, A. M. and Yung, M. (1996). Cryptovirology: Extortion-Based Security Threats and Countermeasures. *IEEE Symposium on Security and Privacy*, pp. 129–140. doi: 10.1109/SECPRI.1996.502676. ISBN 0-8186-7417-2.

30. Schofield, J. (2016, July 28). How Can I Remove a Ransomware Infection? *The Guardian*. Retrieved https://www.theguardian.com /technology/askjack/2016/jul/28/how-can-i-remove-ransomware -infection

31. Mimoso, M. (2016, March 28). Petya Ransomware Master File Table Encryption. threatpost.com. Retrieved https://threatpost .com/petya-ransomware-encrypts-master-file-table/117024/

32. Luna, J. (2016, September 21). Mamba Ransomware Encrypts Your Hard Drive, Manipulates the Boot Process. Neowin. Retrieved from https://www.neowin.net/news/mamba-ransomware-encrypts -your-hard-drive-manipulates-the-boot-process/

33. Cameron, D. (2017, May 13). Today's Massive Ransomware Attack Was Mostly Preventable; Here's How to Avoid It. Gizmodo. Retrieved from https://www.gizmodo.com.au/2017/05/todays -massive-ransomware-attack-was-mostly-preventable-heres-how -to-avoid-it/

34. Wikipedia. (2021). Ransomware. Retrieved from https://en.wikipedia .org/wiki/Ransomware

35. Statista. (2021). Number of Newly Discovered Ransomware Families Worldwide from 2015 to 2020. Retrieved from https:// www.statista.com/statistics/701029/number-of-newly-added-ransom ware-families-worldwide/

36. Robertson, J. and Turton, W. (2021, July 4). Mass Ransomware Hack Used IT Software Flaws, Researchers Say. Retrieved from https://

finance.yahoo.com/news/mass-ransomware-hack-used-software
-183846563.html

37. safeatlast. (2021). 22 Shocking Ransomware Statistics for Cyber-security in 2021. Blog. Retrieved from https://safeatlast.co/blog
/ransomware-statistics/

38. Kaspersky. (2019, August 19). What Is an Advanced Persistent Threat (APT)? Retrieved from https://www.kaspersky.com/resource-center
/definitions/advanced-persistent-threats

39. Cisco. (2019, August 11). What Is an Advanced Persistent Threat (APT)? Retrieved from https://www.cisco.com/c/en/us/products
/security/advanced-persistent-threat.html

40. Maloney, S. (2018, November 9). What Is an Advanced Persistent Threat (APT)? Blog. Retrieved from https://www.cybereason.com
/blog/advanced-persistent-threat-apt

41. FireEye. (2019, August 11). M-Trends Cyber Security Trend. Retrieved from https://www.fireeye.com/current-threats/annual
-threat-report/mtrends.html

42. FireEye. (2019, August 11). Cyber Threats to the Financial Services and Insurance Industries (PDF). Archived from the original (PDF). Retrieved from https://web.archive.org/web/20190811091624/
https://www.fireeye.com/content/dam/fireeye-www/solutions/pdfs
/ib-finance.pdf

43. FireEye. (2019, August 11). Cyber Threats to the Retail and Consumer Goods Industry (PDF). Archived from the original (PDF) on August 11, 2019. Retrieved from https://web.archive
.org/web/20190811091947/https://www.fireeye.com/content/dam
/fireeye-www/global/en/solutions/pdfs/ib-retail-consumer.pdf

44. Symantec. (2018, May 8). Advanced Persistent Threats: A Symantec Perspective (PDF). Archived from the original (PDF). Retrieved from https://www.symantec.com/content/en/us/enterprise/white_papers
/b-advanced_persistent_threats_WP_21215957.en-us.pdf

45. FireEye. (2019, August 11). M-Trends Cyber Security Trend. Retrieved from https://www.fireeye.com/current-threats/annual
-threat-report/mtrends.html

46. Wikipedia. (2001). Advanced Persistent Threat. Retrieved from https://en.m.wikipedia.org/wiki/Advanced_persistent_threat

47. Wikipedia. (2021). Cozy Bear. Retrieved from https://en.m.wikipedia
.org/wiki/Cozy_Bear

48. FireEye. (2021). Advanced Persistent Threat Groups—Who's Who of Cyber Threat Actors. Retrieved from https://www.fireeye.com /current-threats/apt-groups.html

49. Nichols, S. (2021, July 2). Russia Using Kubernetes Cluster for Brute-Force Attacks. Retrieved from https://searchsecurity.techtarget .com/news/252503482/Russia-using-Kubernetes-cluster-for-brute -force-attacks?utm_campaign=20210707_NSA+sounds+alarm+on +Russian+container-based+attacks%3B+Plus%2C+REvil+ransom ware+returns&utm_medium=EM&utm_source=NLN&track=NL -1820&ad=939572&asrc=EM_NLN_169456182

50. Clarke, R. A. and Knake, R. K. (2010). *Cyber War: The Next Threat to National Security and What to Do About It.* New York (NY): HarperCollins Publishers.

51. *The Economist.* (2010, July 1). Cyberwar: War in the Fifth Domain. Retrieved from https://www.economist.com/briefing/2010/07/01 /war-in-the-fifth-domain

52. U.S. Department of Defense Strategy for Operating in Cyberspace. (2011, July), p. 3. Retrieved from https://csrc.nist.gov/CSRC /media/Projects/ISPAB/documents/DOD-Strategy-for-Operating-in -Cyberspace.pdf

53. Ibid.

54. thinktechadvisors. (2021). Proactive vs. Reactive Security. Retrieved from https://thinktechadvisors.com/2020/01/proactive -vs-reactive-cybersecurity/

55. Jelen, S. (2021). Reactive vs. Proactive Security: Which Is Better? Blog. Retrieved from https://securitytrails.com/blog/reactive-vs -proactive-security

56. Fasulo, P. (2021, May 19). Reactive vs. Proactive Cybersecurity: 7 Benefits. Blog. Retrieved from https://securityscorecard.com/blog /reactive-vs-proactive-cybersecurity

57. Crowdstrike. (2020). Crowdstrike Services Cyber Front Lines Report: Observations from the Front Lines of Incident Response and Proactive Services in 2019 and Insights That Matter for 2020. Retrieved from https://www.techrepublic.com/index.php /publisher/6290336/index.php/resource-library/whitepapers/crowd strike-services-cyber-front-lines-report-2019/

58. Crowdstrike. (2020). Press Releases: New CrowdStrike Report Finds an Increase in Cyber Adversaries Turning to Business

Disruption as Main Attack Objective. Retrieved from https://www
.crowdstrike.com/press-releases/report-finds-business-disruption-is
-main-objective-of-adversaries/

59. Kosutic, D. (2018). Asset Management According to ISO 27001:
How to Handle an Asset Register/Asset Inventory. Retrieved
from https://advisera.com/27001academy/knowledgebase/how
-to-handle-asset-register-asset-inventory-according-to-iso-27001/

60. Ibid.

61. Fancher, D., Gelinne, J., and Mossburg, E. (2021). Deloitte.
Perspectives: Seven Hidden Costs of a Cyberattack. CFO Insights.
Retrieved from https://www2.deloitte.com/us/en/pages/finance
/articles/cfo-insights-seven-hidden-costs-cyberattack.html

62. Mossburg, E., Gelinne, J., and Calzada, H. (2016). Deloitte. Beneath
the Surface of a Cyberattack: A Deeper Look at Business Impacts.
Cyber. Retrieved from https://www2.deloitte.com/content/dam
/Deloitte/us/Documents/risk/us-risk-beneath-the-surface-of-a-cyber
-attack.pdf

63. Gelinne, J., Mossburg, E., and Fancher, D. (2016, July 15). The
Hidden Costs of an IP Breach: Cyber Theft and the Loss of
Intellectual Property. *Deloitte Review*. Issue 19. Retrieved from
https://www2.deloitte.com/us/en/insights/deloitte-review/issue-19
/loss-of-intellectual-property-ip-breach.html

64. Aries Security. (2020, October 18). 6 Risks of Not Conducting Continuous Cybersecurity Training. Retrieved from https://www.aries
security.com/6-risks-of-not-conducting-continuous-cybersecurity
-training/

65. Lobo, S. (2019, March 31). Understanding the Cost of a Cybersecurity
Attack: The Losses Organizations Face. Retrieved from https://hub
.packtpub.com/understanding-the-cost-of-a-cybersecurity-attack
-the-losses-organizations-face/

66. Palmer, D. (2018, February 21). Cybercrime Drains $600 Billion a
Year from the Global Economy, Says Report. Retrieved from https://
www.zdnet.com/article/cybercrime-drains-600-billion-a-year-from
-the-global-economy-says-report/

67. Lobo, S. (2019, March 31). Understanding The Cost of a Cybersecurity
Attack: The Losses Organizations Face. Retrieved from https://hub
.packtpub.com/understanding-the-cost-of-a-cybersecurity-attack
-the-losses-organizations-face/

68. Mossburg, E., Gelinne, J., and Calzada, H. (2016). Deloitte. Beneath the Surface of a Cyberattack: A Deeper Look at Business Impacts. Cyber. Retrieved from https://www2.deloitte.com/content/dam /Deloitte/us/Documents/risk/us-risk-beneath-the-surface-of-a-cyber -attack.pdf
69. Ibid.
70. Fancher, D., Gelinne, J., and Mossburg, E. (2021). Deloitte. Perspectives: Seven Hidden Costs of a Cyberattack. CFO Insights. Retrieved from https://www2.deloitte.com/us/en/pages/finance /articles/cfo-insights-seven-hidden-costs-cyberattack.html
71. Deloitte. (2018). CEO and Board Risk Management Survey Illuminating a Path Forward on Strategic Risk. Retrieved from https://www2.deloitte.com/us/en/pages/risk/articles/download-the -ceo-and-board-risk-management-survey.html?id=us:2em:3na:ceo survey:awa:adv:101018&sfid
72. Eisenstein, L. (2019, August 23). Cybersecurity and Managing Reputational Risk. Blog. Retrieved from https://www.boardeffect .com/blog/cybersecurity-managing-reputational-risk/
73. Black Kite. (2020, August 26). Reputational Cyber Risk—How to Avoid Business Lost. Retrieved from https://blackkite.com /reputational-cyber-risk-how-to-avoid-business-lost/
74. TitanHQ Web Titan. (2019, January 25). New Research Reveals Extent of Reputation Loss After a Cyberattack. Retrieved from https://www.spamtitan.com/web-filtering/new-research -reveals-extent-of-reputation-loss-after-a-cyberattack/
75. Lobo, S. (2019, March 31). Understanding the Cost of a Cybersecurity Attack: The Losses Organizations Face. Retrieved from https://hub .packtpub.com/understanding-the-cost-of-a-cybersecurity-attack -the-losses-organizations-face/

# Chapter 5

# Governing Cybersecurity Risk

## 5.1 INTRODUCTION

Imagine managing your organization's sales, growth, profits, expenses, or performance with only quarterly or yearly reports by experts who use terms and metrics in a language that is foreign to all but those with specific skills and training. A business today cannot be managed in this way, and, in fact, most modern business organizations operate with near real-time (NRT) information in most critical areas. Leadership reports use well-understood metrics and terms that are continuously updated to highlight both absolute measures and trends. One does not need to be a sales expert to understand a Salesforce.com report.

## 5.2 THE EXCEPTION OF CYBERSECURITY GOVERNANCE

The C-suite, private equity firms, and boards of directors (BoD) demand current and well-understood information to drive critical decisions and manage risk. Whether the organization is a business, a university, or a non-profit, cybersecurity is a top-of-the-house concern. Why is cybersecurity risk governance the exception? Today, cybersecurity is not governed in the same way as other significant risks are governed. This is detrimental to the organization.

Leadership must be continuously engaged in governing cybersecurity risk because:

- It's a tax that can't be avoided.
- Its harm has no limits.
- Threats and threat actors are continuously evolving.
- Threat actors use automation to increase the number of targets.
- Connections with vendors and customers drive risk.
- The surface area of harm is ever increasing.
- Not all threat actors act rationally.
- Every organization has significant cybersecurity incidents; there are no exceptions.

Given the ubiquity of cybersecurity risk and the unlimited potential harm, leadership must get more engaged. This does not mean that leadership must become cybersecurity geeks. Rather, cybersecurity risk must be understood, monitored, and managed like other significant business risks.

Although hundreds of billions of dollars a year are spent on monitoring and preventing cybersecurity events, cybersecurity governance has not moved forward. Leadership is poorly equipped with dated information that is rarely correlated to business risk to properly provide cybersecurity governance. It's an obsolete island of analog information in a digital world.

CYBERPHOS delivers a continuously updated dashboard and key metrics to guide leadership's understanding of the organization's cybersecurity posture, its progress, and questions that engage both leadership and security experts in a common framework.

## 5.3 THE CHALLENGES OF MANAGING CYBERSECURITY RISK

Most organizations manage cybersecurity risk with infrequent reports anchored in technical jargon, little direct interaction between the chief information security officer (CISO) and leadership, annual assessments from an outside review group, and other point-in-time assessments. This approach leads to large gaps in understanding and governance decisions with incomplete information and poor synergy between business decisions and their cybersecurity impact. This approach is the equivalent of using a yearly balance sheet to derive a current cash flow statement. How can you make forward-looking decisions with dated and incomplete information?

This occurs in a business and technical environment that is adding computing technology and information at an exponential rate, connecting more and more devices that interact with each other, and information processing and access that is NRT 24/7. The surface area of the meta-enterprise, the organization, its vendors, and customers, is ever expanding. Although these trends in technology and information drive business growth, it also comes at a cost of an increased surface area for cyber threat actors.

## 5.3.1 Traditional Security Assessments

Annual assessments are point-in-time measures of cybersecurity posture that vary widely in fidelity and accuracy. Even an excellent review in no way guarantees that a negative cybersecurity event is not currently in play or will not happen soon. Just as looking at a bank balance today is not an indicator of that bank balance a week from now.

In addition, it is difficult to find an entity that will provide an independent assessment without restrictions or agendas to drive follow-on work. Accounting firms have independence restrictions that prohibit them from disclosing any finding that harms their audit clients. Imagine a cybersecurity assessment where you are prohibited from disclosing cybersecurity concerns with your network or software providers. Most firms typically conduct cybersecurity assessments to drive follow-on work; thus, they are motivated to find issues that align with their service offerings. These "gold standard" reviews are flawed. If the assessment was perfect and actionable, it is still a point in time. New threats and new threat actors will emerge tomorrow.

Assessments rely on significant human bias, both by the assessor and the assessed. We have been on both sides of this process, and we have seen that it is relatively easy for an experienced assessor to achieve a higher rating, whereas a less-experienced assessor could achieve a lower rating even if everything else regarding cybersecurity in the organization was equal. As Ray Dalio detailed in his book *Principles: Life and Work*,[1] trusted systems must be developed that remove human bias to enable accurate decisions.

### 5.3.2 Leadership Challenges

Leadership is organized to address the issues of the past, present, future, and tangible regulatory items. Look at any board or advisory committee and you have accounting, finance, marketing, and operations expertise. Few in leadership have the cybersecurity expertise to guide and govern this critical challenge. In response, some boards have added a technology expert to help with this issue. Although a logical step, this is often counterproductive.

What often happens is that the cybersecurity expert dives into the weeds with the CISO, leaving the rest of the leadership group lost and ill-informed to provide proper guidance. Cybersecurity metrics and indicators should be presented in business terms in order to facilitate business discussions with leadership.

### 5.3.3 Infinity and Beyond

Most leadership challenges have finite risks and rewards. Allocate a fixed number of resources to resolve a manufacturing or accounting issue. Even when damages are difficult to assess, organizations negotiate fines and other fixed remedies with regulators to drive certainty for the organization.

Cybersecurity is a different challenge in that an organization can spend its entire budget on cybersecurity and still have the probability of a significant compromise. This is coupled with threat actors such as nation-states that will pursue an agenda despite the cost. Ask Sony what the cost of angering North Korea was. No amount of cybersecurity insurance or other hedge mechanism can prevent a catastrophic outcome from a motivated advisory. The downside risk of a significant cybersecurity event approaches infinity.

## 5.3.4 Chief Information Security Officer (CISO)

As the title suggests, in most large organizations, there is a specific individual and team charged with keeping the organization secure. Most CISOs are technologists who have gravitated to cybersecurity through interest or government background. They are comfortable with the deep technical knowledge required to monitor and manage an organization's cybersecurity posture. There are thousands of tools and services focused on the CISO world to monitor and manage the security technology, information, and access. These tools are comfortable to those in the CISO world but use terms, measures, and reporting that sound like Klingon[*] to business leaders. "Our firewalls are pinged a million times a day." Is this a good thing or a bad thing? How does this relate to business risk?

*If you don't know how a business works, how can you protect it?*

One of the dirty secrets in the CISO world is that relatively few have deep knowledge of the business and its industry, which they are charged to protect. Many have a government or technology infrastructure background that is devoid of business knowledge. Banks don't take a trader and make them a CISO, and an electric utility does not take a production manager and make them a CISO. The gold standard for CISO certification—the Certified Information Systems Security Professional (CISSP)—does not have a business-knowledge section. Instead, it requires memorizing

---

[*] Retrieved from https://en.wikipedia.org/wiki/Klingon_language

esoteric points related to data encryption, computing infrastructure, network traffic, etc. There is no requirement to understand how the front-, middle-, and back-office workers interact with each other.

Essentially, a CISO is a victim of complexity and managing that is one of the key elements of cybertax that is managed through the CYBERPHOS solution.

### 5.3.5 Below the Surface

Hidden costs (below the surface) were touched on in Section 4.3.3.5: Economic Damage. As stated previously, the research showed that the direct costs commonly associated with data breaches were far less significant than the "hidden" costs. An abbreviated hidden cost list and short description of what is provided in the Deloitte™ document[2] follow:

- **Insurance premium increases.** Insurance premium increases are the additional costs an insured entity might incur to purchase or renew cyber risk insurance policies following a cyber incident.
- **Increased cost to raise debt.** Increased cost to raise debt occurs when, as a result of a drop in credit rating, the victim organization faces higher interest rates for borrowed capital, either when raising debt or when renegotiating existing debt.
- **Operational disruption or destruction.** The impact of operational disruption or destruction is a highly variable cost category that includes losses tied to manipulation or alteration of normal business operations and costs associated with rebuilding operational capabilities.
- **Lost value of customer relationships.** During an initial period immediately following a breach, it can be hard to track and quantify how many customers are lost. Economists and marketing teams approach this challenge by attaching a

"value" to each customer or member to quantify how much the business must invest to acquire that customer or member.

- **Value of lost contract revenue.** Value of lost contract revenue includes revenue and ultimate income loss, as well as lost future opportunity associated with contracts that are terminated as a result of a cyber incident.
- **Devaluation of trade name.** Devaluation of trade name is an intangible cost category referring to the loss in value of the names, marks, or symbols an organization uses to distinguish its products and services.
- **Loss of intellectual property (IP).** Loss of IP is an intangible cost associated with loss of exclusive control over trade secrets, copyrights, investment plans, and other proprietary and confidential information that can lead to loss of competitive advantage, loss of revenue, and lasting and potentially irreparable economic damage to the company.

## 5.3.6 Emerging Threats

We believe that the following emerging threats will be issues to contend with for the foreseeable future:

- **Brute-Force Frustrations.** Brute-force efforts are also back in fashion. The attackers behind this and other cybersecurity trends recognize the potential of a distributed denial-of-service (DDoS) attack in bringing down corporate networks.[3]
- **Fileless Frameworks.** Fileless malware and ransomware attacks will continue to plague entities in 2022. These threats are designed to bypass familiar detection controls and infiltrate key systems by "living off the land"—using approved platforms or software tools that already exist within corporate networks.[4]
- **Impact of Remote Work: New Threats and Solutions.** It's only a matter of time before attackers compromise multiple,

insecure home networks and simultaneously manufacture a massive-scale breach of critical systems and services.[5]

- **New Challenges from Ransomware.** Ransomware is one of the most common threats to any organization's data security, and this threat will continue to increase and evolve as a top cybersecurity trend beyond 2022.[6]

- **Increased Attacks on Cloud Services.** With the rapid and widespread adoption of remote work following COVID-19, the necessity for cloud-based services and infrastructure increased drastically.[7]

- **Personally Identifiable Information (PII) Attacks.** With the growing number of high-profile cyber attacks exposing millions of PII records, concerns about data privacy, management, and security will continue to skyrocket.[8]

- **Increased Need for Cybersecurity Professionals.** Finding well-trained cybersecurity professionals has historically been a challenge across all industries, but the continued shift to and dependence on a more distributed workforce is creating a more critical need for them in 2022.[9]

- **Insider Threats on the Rise.** This is especially true as organizations continue to hire remote-only employees who are scattered across the world, and who they may have hired only after meeting them virtually.[10]

- **Critical Need for Real-Time Data Visibility.** Although many executives are managing cybersecurity risks for some aspects of their organization, their efforts are weakened without a comprehensive picture of the company's entire technological landscape. This results in weakened risk assessment programs, since they're often based on inventories that lack a full and clear picture of the threat landscape.[11]

- **Increasing Cyber Attack Surface.** 2022 has seen one of the highest increases in attack surface, and the next half of the year and beyond is expected to witness more expansion.[12]

- **Critical Infrastructure Threats Will Increase.** Cyber attacks have become widespread across the transportation, healthcare, and energy sectors, and this has the potential to snowball into a more serious issue if left unchecked.[13]

- **Chief Information Security Officers (CISOs).** There is an increased need for CISOs who can communicate from both a business and technical perspective.

### 5.3.7 Cybertax

As stated at the beginning of the book, cybertax has nothing to do with the traditional compulsory contribution of revenue to a government entity. Cybertax is the percentage of effort and resources used to prove cybersecurity posture to others (partners, regulators, auditors), which takes effort away from providing cybersecurity capability. Time spent **proving** cybersecurity posture to auditors, regulators, business partners, and others takes time away from **doing** cybersecurity. This factor will have a disproportionate effect on the cybertax score. A high cybertax score is extremely detrimental to cybersecurity capability.

### 5.4 SUMMARY

This chapter has given a high-level overview of cybersecurity risks, threats, governance, and management challenges that currently affect the meta-enterprise. For the sake of this book, the meta-enterprise is your organization and all those whom you connect to, including partners, vendors, customers, technology providers, etc. Chapter 5 is provided for background and to establish the value provided by the solution that we will describe in Chapter 6.

Managing cybersecurity risks should be achieved like other key business risks using frequency, key metrics, and thoughtful governance to drive effectiveness and measurable improvements. Ownership must be taken regarding leadership decisions that impact cybersecurity, while engaging your cybersecurity team proactively to assess the impact of key business decisions on cybersecurity. Finally, you must strive to proactively build cybersecurity into all aspects of the meta-enterprise rather than attempting to reactively deal with cybersecurity issues.

## REFERENCES

1. Dalio, R. (2017). *Principles: Life and Work*. New York (NY): Simon & Schuster.
2. Fancher, D., Gelinne, J., and Mossburg, E. (2021). Deloitte Perspectives: Seven Hidden Costs of a Cyberattack—CFO Insights. Retrieved from https://www2.deloitte.com/us/en/pages/finance/articles/cfo-insights-seven-hidden-costs-cyberattack.html
3. Bonderud, D. (2021, March 3). Cybersecurity Trends and Emerging Threats in 2021. Retrieved from https://securityintelligence.com/articles/cybersecurity-trends-and-emerging-threats-2021/
4. Ibid.
5. Panda—A WatchGuard Brand. (2021, April 12). 11 Emerging Cybersecurity Trends in 2021. Retrieved from https://www.pandasecurity.com/en/mediacenter/tips/cybersecurity-trends/
6. Ibid.
7. Ibid.
8. Ibid.
9. Ibid.
10. Ibid.
11. Ibid.
12. LIV. (2021, May 10). 3 Emerging Cybersecurity Trends in 2021. Retrieved from https://roboticsandautomationnews.com/2021/05/10/3-emerging-cybersecurity-trends-in-2021/43138/
13. Ibid.

# Chapter 6

# Solution—CYBERPHOS

## 6.1 INTRODUCTION

After years of managing cybersecurity risk using traditional methods and measures, we realized that the disconnect between leadership and the chief information security officer (CISO) will never be bridged this way. CYBERPHOS will bridge the chasm between the two groups so that cybersecurity can be managed rationally and effectively. Although frameworks such as the NIST *Framework for Improving Critical Infrastructure Cybersecurity* are useful tools, they fail to bridge the significant gap in understanding between leadership and the CISO.

Imagine a yearly gathering of thousands of cybersecurity practitioners seeking products and solutions to the ever-daunting problem of protecting their organization from every type of threat actor. You don't have to wonder. Just head to San Francisco's Moscone Convention Center with 30,000 other security professionals during the yearly RSA Security Conference. You will be overwhelmed by the thousands of solutions pitched to solve specific cybersecurity challenges. Just as in golf, there is no game in a box, there is no vendor solution to completely protect your organization from motivated threat actors. But that does not stop the vendors from trying to convince you that there is a solution in a box. The result is that most organizations have too many tools, not enough talent, and mixed priorities, which challenges delivering a good cybersecurity posture.

CYBERPHOS focuses on seven key aspects (the Seven C's) of cybersecurity risk governance. The Seven C's use the foundational components of complexity, capability, and competency coupled with the ability to compare, conceptualize, and determine cost of potential changes. The last component, continuous, is a quality associated with all information inputs. By measuring and analyzing cybersecurity using the Seven C's, an organization is positioned to deploy resources effectively and reduce the cybertax.

## 6.2 THE SEVEN C'S

There are many cybersecurity frameworks and assessments that are derived from the ISO® 27001 standard. These assessments are useful for cybersecurity practitioners but do little to help leadership understand and manage cybersecurity risk. Leadership in this context is defined as the key business owners, C-suite executives, and the board of directors. These frameworks do little to correlate business complexity and cybersecurity capability into a competency score that guides leadership attention, issue probing, and governance for the cybersecurity team and its services.

The other significant gap in the current frameworks is that they measure cybersecurity effectiveness as a point-in-time exercise, typically annually. Every other significant risk to the organization is measured and monitored with near real-time (NRT) information and metrics. Think of sales, growth, finances, human resources, and supply chain, all of which are measured, monitored, and analyzed with NRT information. Why is cybersecurity risk, which is potentially unlimited, measured and governed infrequently?

Organizations strive to improve their cybersecurity posture in a world in which cybersecurity threats and vectors are constantly evolving. Think of cybersecurity posture as the overall cybersecurity competency score. Infrequent measurements of cybersecurity risk are inadequate in a world in which the threat actors operate in real time.

The CYBERPHOS Seven C's formulas and method measures organization complexity, capability, and competency. These three vectors are the foundational components of the Seven C's methodology. Using the data from the foundational components, the methodology enables the ability to conceptualize change, compare against peers, and model the cost of change. The frequency of information refresh, continuous, is quality and a metric applied to the foundational components. The more frequently information is updated, the better the Continuous score and the better the method works.

The CYBERPHOS method for continuously measuring cybersecurity—complexity, capability, and competency using conceptualization, comparison, and cost—enables leadership to understand their organization's cybersecurity risks, its ability to address these risks, and its overall effectiveness in combating the continuous risks from cybersecurity threats. CYBERPHOS refers to this method as the Seven C's. The Seven C's are described in the following sections.

## 6.2.1 Complexity

This is a long-overlooked factor influencing effective cybersecurity. Few organizations measure or monitor business and technology complexity for its impact on cybersecurity posture. For example, it stands to reason that it is easier to update and manage software patches for two operating systems than it is for a dozen. Unpatched software and operating systems have greater cybersecurity risks than systems with the latest patches correctly installed. Most organizations are driven by short-term cost and acquire a heterogeneous collection of technology and business methods. Although this may be optimal in the short term, it makes providing effective cybersecurity more difficult. Complexity is not limited to technology. It measures business, location, and workforce complexity as well.

Complexity is calculated across a number of dimensions that make it difficult to provide effective cybersecurity. Although CISOs rarely influence organization complexity, their responsibility to find and prevent cybersecurity issues are greatly impacted by their organization's complexity. The scoring methodology for complexity is outlined in Table 6.1.

**Table 6.1  Scoring Methodology for Complexity**

| Top Level Score | Support Score | Score Components | Score Range |
|---|---|---|---|
| **Technology** | Platforms | • Servers<br>• Data<br>• Cloud | 0–1.0 |
| | Personal technology | • Personal computers<br>• Tablets<br>• Mobile devices | 0–1.0 |
| | Internet of Things (IoT) | • Security<br>• Environmental<br>• Interactions | 0–1.0 |
| **Identities** | People | • Employees<br>• Contractors | 0–1.0 |
| | System | • Internal<br>• External | 0–1.0 |
| **Locations** | Location complexity | • Main locations<br>• Minor locations<br>• Satellite locations | 0–1.0 |

The formulas for complexity are:

Servers + Personal Technology + Data Platforms + Cloud Platforms = Platforms Score

Human Identities + System Identities = Identity Score

Major Locations + Minor Locations + Satellite Locations = Location Score

Platforms + Identities + Locations = Complexity Score

Shadow IT Budget/Total IT Budget = IT Control Score

Platforms, identities, and locations will also be measured over time—both the trend and direction of change for these critical factors affecting a good cybersecurity posture.

Although scoring criteria will change over time, both on an absolute scale and a relative scale as compared to peer organizations, the best scores approach zero.

## 6.2.2 Capability

This important factor examines the technology, methods, and people required to provide cybersecurity to the organization.

Although most organizations have cybersecurity capabilities, they are rarely balanced and focused on protecting the most critical assets. Additionally, the cybersecurity team seldom has detailed knowledge about how the company operates from the front, middle, and back office. This point is verified by the number of former government cybersecurity professionals in industry. They have a keen grasp of threat actors and threat vectors but are ill-equipped to understand how to protect the complex internal workings of the organization they are charged to protect. The capability portion of this method measures the ability and alignment of resources to protect the organization's significant assets and capabilities on an ongoing basis.

Capability is the measure of the organization's ability to proactively and reactively address cybersecurity issues and responsibilities. This is measured against internal policy goals as well as relative to peers. Capability factors include the following:

- Technology footprint
- Ability of the cybersecurity team to effectively use the technology
- Skills and industry knowledge of the cybersecurity team
- Cybersecurity interaction with organization leadership

This score has a factor, Proving, which will increase the overall score proportionate to the level of Proving provided by the cybersecurity team. Proving is the percentage of effort and resources used to prove cybersecurity posture to others (partners, regulators, auditors) that takes effort away from providing cybersecurity capability. Time spent **Proving** cybersecurity posture to auditors, regulators, business partners, and others takes time away from **Doing** cybersecurity. This factor will have a disproportionate effect on the score. A high Proving score is detrimental to cybersecurity capability as it diverts resources from Doing.

A perfect capability score does not mean that the organization's cybersecurity posture is perfect; it merely indicates that the resources are aligned well to deliver effective cybersecurity services. No organization is immune to cybersecurity incidents. The scoring methodology for capability is outlined in Table 6.2.

### Table 6.2 Scoring Methodology for Capability

| Top Level Score | Support Score | Score Components | Score Range |
|---|---|---|---|
| **Technology tools** | Hardware | • Tools<br>• Resources required<br>• Resource deficit | 0–1.0 |
| | Software | • Tools<br>• Resources required<br>• Resource deficit | 0–1.0 |
| | Software as a Service (SaaS) | • Services<br>• Resources required<br>• Resource deficit | 0–1.0 |
| **Team** | People | • Skills<br>• Industry Knowledge | 0–1.0 |
| | Leadership access | • Frequency<br>• Time<br>• Quality vs. overhead | 0–1.0 |
| **Proving** | Reviews | • Vendor<br>• Internal<br>• External | 0–1.0 |
| | Significant incidents | • Time away from normal tasks | |

The formulas for capability are:

Tool Hours Required − Resources Available = Tool Resource Deficit

Software Hours Required − Resources Available = Software Resource Deficit

SaaS Hours Required − Resources Available = SaaS Resource Deficit

Team Skill Score

Team Industry Knowledge Source

Cybersecurity Leadership Access Score

Total Team Hours/Total Proving Hours = Proving Factor

Proving Factor = TBD (The Proving factor will increase the competency score and will be adjusted over time as data and research indicates how debilitating the Proving is to competency.)

All of these factors will have both an absolute score as well as a trend and trend direction score. Trend indicates change over time of the score so that leadership can identify both good and bad trends addressing key cybersecurity issues.

### 6.2.3 Competency

The third foundational leg of this method is competency. This measures the effective execution of cybersecurity across the organization. Good cybersecurity can be measured, for example, as follows:

- Are we finding new issues and not repeating issues?
- Are we finding issues sooner?
- Are we spending more time providing cybersecurity rather than proving it to others?

Competency measures factors such as these and others to determine both absolute competency and the trend and velocity of the trend over time. This information informs leadership as to areas of good cybersecurity competency and those areas requiring leadership attention.

Competency is the third and most important foundation component of our assessment vectors. Competency refers to the effectiveness of the cybersecurity posture of the organization. This is measured in both absolute terms and in terms of change velocity and direction of each factor. For example, a good repeat issues score in incident resolution would see the change in incidents decreasing while their effective closure is increasing.

Effectiveness is also diluted (harmed) as obligations are added in the form of:

- Additional audits
- Additional regulations
- Acquisitions
- New product and service lines
- New technology
- New threat vectors

Repeat issues are weighted more than new issues, as repeating issues indicate a lack of properly remediating the root cause of the issue. The scoring methodology for effectiveness is outlined in Table 6.3.

**Table 6.3  Scoring Methodology for Effectiveness**

| Top Level Score | Support Score | Score Components | Score Range |
|---|---|---|---|
| **Incidents** | New | • Tools<br>• Resources required<br>• Resource deficit | 0–1.0 |
| | Repeat | • Issues<br>• Issues resolved | 0–1.0 |
| | Vendor | • Issues<br>• Issues resolved<br>• Team overhead<br>• Vendor score | 0–1.0 |
| **Asset Correlation** | Asset/resource correlation | • Resource distributions<br>• Asset value | 0–1.0 |
| | Emerging obligations | • Internal<br>• External | 0–1.0 |
| **Dilutions** | Reviews | • Vendor<br>• Internal<br>• External | 0–1.0 |
| | Significant incidents | • Time away from normal tasks | |

The formulas for competency are:

New Issues/Timely Issue Resolution = New Issue Score
New Issue Trend and Velocity = New Issues/Time
Repeat Issues/Timely Issue Resolution = Repeat Issue Score
Repeat Issue Trend and Velocity = Repeat Issues/Time
Vendor Issues/Timely Issue Resolution = Vendor Issue Score
Vendor Issue Trend and Velocity = Vendor Issues/Time
Reviews + New Obligations + Incident Time = Dilutions

## 6.2.4 Comparison

CYBERPHOS puts your organization's cybersecurity posture in context by organization size and industry. Although each organization must determine its own cybersecurity goals and capabilities, it's often helpful to understand how one's organization compares to similar organizations. CYBERPHOS anonymizes comparison data to deliver valuable reference information while respecting an organization's identity.

### 6.2.5 Conceptualization

Using the CYBERPHOS *what if* capability, organizations can analyze and understand how changes in one area will impact the overall cybersecurity posture score. This method provides factors that can be adjusted to determine the impact of potential changes or improvements. For example, a company moving from a divergent set of laptops to a single laptop standard would see their complexity score reduce and increase their cybersecurity posture. This feature can also be used to analyze the impact of an acquisition or divestiture.

Once the baseline state of the organization is determined by the CYBERPHOS modeling tool, there are *what if* scenarios that can be used to represent changes to complexity, competency, and capability. This tool lets the user manipulate factors to determine the best way to improve cybersecurity across one dimension or the entire security posture. Conceptualization can also be used to model the effect of changes such as acquisitions, expansions, divestitures, and other significant changes. Rarely is the impact to cybersecurity posture contemplated as part of significant organization decisions. CYBERPHOS enables this analysis for consideration.

### 6.2.6 Cost

In combination with the CYBERPHOS conceptualization tool, organizations can understand the approximate cost of investments that could reduce complexity, improve capabilities, and increase data frequency in order to drive improved competency. Cost is determined both in dollars and calendar time. Using the laptop example above, this tool calculates the total cost of changing from a heterogeneous population of laptops to a homogeneous state. This tool comes with a standard set of Cost metrics that can be customized by a particular organization.

Working in concert with the conceptualization tool, an organization can understand the approximate Cost of proposed changes to the organization along the complexity, capability, and competency dimensions. These cost approximations help estimate the impact of changes to improve cybersecurity, changes to the size and scope of the organization, and changes imposed by customers or regulators. CYBERPHOS has built-in cost factors that can be customized with an individual organization's cost factors.

Cost includes the concept of calendar time; this will also impact business decisions or the impact of meeting customer or regulatory demands.

### 6.2.7 Continuous

The Seven C's method does not determine the appropriate amount of risk an organization should tolerate. It does, however, help leadership understand key factors influencing their organization's cybersecurity risk and how to improve its cybersecurity posture. Similar to other key risks, leadership must apply resources to deliver a risk level appropriate for the organization and its partners and customers.

This method highlights factors influencing cybersecurity complexity, capability, and competency. Not only will this method provide an absolute and peer-relevant complexity score, but it will also indicate which factors influence the score in impact order. This enables leadership to focus on issues that impact and improve cybersecurity posture. This is driven by alerts built into the tool that highlight areas requiring leadership's attention.

The Seven C's Method also monitors trends both positive and negative so leadership can assess the organization's ability to find and respond to the ever-changing spectrum of cybersecurity threats. For example, a trend highlighting that similar cybersecurity exploits are increasing point to an organization that is ineffective at learning from previous exploits and unable to develop a wholistic solution. A trend that demonstrates the organization is finding cybersecurity incidents faster highlights an improving aspect of competency.

Continuous is calculated from the data feeds required to calculate complexity, capability, and competency. The more frequently

**Table 6.4  Scoring Methodology for Complexity**

| Top Level Score | Support Score | Score Components | Score Range |
|---|---|---|---|
| Technology | Platforms | • Servers<br>• Data<br>• Cloud | 0–1.0 |
|  | Personal technology | • Personal Computers<br>• Tablets<br>• Mobile Devices | 0–1.0 |
|  | Internet of Things (IoT) | • Security<br>• Environmental<br>• Interactions | 0–1.0 |
| Identities | People | • Employees<br>• Contractors | 0–1.0 |
|  | System | • Internal<br>• External | 0–1.0 |
| Locations | Location complexity | • Main locations<br>• Minor locations<br>• Satellite locations | 0–1.0 |

The formulas for continuous are:

Servers + Personal Technology + Data Platforms + Cloud Platforms = Platforms Score

Human Identities + System Identities = Identity Score

Major Locations + Minor Locations + Satellite Locations = Location Score

Platforms + Identities + Locations = Complexity Score

Platforms, Identities, and locations will also be measured over time—both the trend and direction of change for these critical factors affecting a good cybersecurity posture.

Although scoring criteria will change over time, both on an absolute scale and a relative scale as compared to peer organizations, the best scores approach zero.

*(See description of Table 6.4 on the following page.)*

information is fed into the CYBERPHOS engine, the closer the continuous score approaches the target of zero, which would correspond to NRT feeds across all relevant inputs. Continuous also scores the quality of the inputs from uncertain to precise. This model accommodates precise estimates and missing data, as this will reflect what is available from most organizations. For example, few organizations capture the precise costs associated with the CYBERPHOS cybertax. This model accommodates guesstimates and well as more precise inputs. At a high level, no information is a 1. Guesstimates and forms input are between 1 and 0.5 and automated feeds score between 0.5 and 0. As with other dimensions of the model, lower scores indicate maturity and precision. The scoring methodology for complexity is outlined in Table 6.4.

## 6.3 KEY CONCERNS

Most organizations manage cybersecurity risk with infrequent reports anchored in technical jargon, annual assessments from an outside review group, and other point-in-time assessments with limited business-relevant risk or real-time and actionable information being provided to senior leadership. This approach leads to large gaps in understanding and governance decisions, with incomplete information and poor synergy between business decisions and their cybersecurity impact. This approach is the equivalent of using a yearly balance sheet to derive a current cash flow statement. How can you make forward-looking decisions with dated and incomplete information?

The situation described above is amplified when a business is growing rapidly in a technical environment that is adding computing technology and information at an exponential rate, connecting more and more devices that interact with each other, and information processing and access that is near real-time, 24/7.

In today's environment, the surface area of the meta-enterprise, the organization, its vendors, and customers is ever expanding. Although these trends in technology and information lubricate business growth, it also comes at the cost of an increased surface area for cyber threat actors.

## 6.3.1 Security Assessments (Traditional)

Annual assessments are point-in-time measures of cybersecurity posture that vary widely in fidelity and accuracy. Even an excellent review in no way guarantees that a negative cybersecurity event is not currently in play or will not happen soon. Just as looking at a bank balance today is not an indicator of that bank balance a week from now.

In addition, it is difficult to find an entity that will provide an independent assessment without restrictions or agendas to drive follow-on work. Accounting firms have independence restrictions that prohibit them from disclosing any finding that harms their audit clients. Imagine a cybersecurity assessment where you are prohibited from disclosing cybersecurity concerns with your network or software providers. Most firms typically conduct cybersecurity assessments to drive follow-on work; thus, they are motivated to find issues that align with their service offerings. These "gold standard" reviews are flawed. If the assessment was perfect and actionable, it is still a point in time. New threats and new threat actors will emerge tomorrow.

Assessments rely on significant human bias, both by the assessor and the assessed. We have been on both sides of this process, and we have seen that it is relatively easy for an experienced assessor to achieve a higher rating, whereas a less-experienced assessor could achieve a lower rating even if everything else regarding cybersecurity in the organization was equal. As Ray Dalio detailed in his book *Principles: Life and Work*,[1] trusted systems must be developed that remove human bias to enable accurate decisions.

### 6.3.2 Leadership Challenges

Leadership is organized to address the issues of the past, present, future, and tangible regulatory items. Look at any board or advisory committee and you have accounting, finance, marketing, and operations expertise. Few in leadership have the cybersecurity expertise to guide and govern this critical challenge. In response, some boards have added a technology expert to help with this issue. Although a logical step, this is often counterproductive.

What often happens is that the cybersecurity expert dives into the weeds with the CISO, leaving the rest of the leadership group lost and ill-informed to provide proper guidance. Cybersecurity metrics and indicators should be presented in business terms in order to facilitate business discussions with leadership.

### 6.3.3 Infinity and Beyond

Most leadership challenges have finite risks and rewards. Allocate a fixed number of resources to resolve a manufacturing or accounting issue. Even when damages are difficult to assess, organizations negotiate fines and other fixed remedies with regulators to drive certainty for the organization.

Cybersecurity is a different challenge in that an organization can spend its entire budget on cybersecurity and still have the probability of a significant compromise. This is coupled with threat actors such as nation-states that will pursue an agenda despite the cost. Ask Sony what the cost of angering North Korea was. No amount of cybersecurity insurance or other hedge mechanism can prevent a catastrophic outcome from a motivated advisory. The downside risk of a significant cybersecurity event approaches infinity.

### 6.3.4 Chief Information Security Officer (CISO)

As the title suggests, in most large organizations, there is a specific individual and team charged with keeping the organization secure. Most CISOs are technologists who have gravitated to cybersecurity through interest or government background. They are comfortable with the deep technical knowledge required to monitor and manage an organization's cybersecurity posture. There are thousands of tools and services focused on the CISO world to monitor and manage the security technology, information, and access. These tools are comfortable to those in the CISO world but use terms, measures, and reporting that sound like Klingon* to business leaders. "Our firewalls are pinged a million times a day." Is this a good thing or a bad thing? How does this relate to business risk?

One of the dirty secrets in the CISO world is that relatively few have deep knowledge of the business and its industry, which they are charged to protect. Many have a government or technology infrastructure background that is devoid of business knowledge. Banks don't take a trader and make them a CISO, and an electric utility does not take a production manager and make them a CISO. The gold standard for CISO certification—the Certified Information Systems Security Professional (CISSP)—does not have a business-knowledge section. Instead, it requires memorizing esoteric points related to data encryption, computing infrastructure, network traffic, etc. There is no requirement to understand how the front-, middle-, and back-office workers interact with each other. *If you don't know how a business works, how can you protect it?*

We anticipate resistance from CISOs as we bridge the chasm, although this pushback is misplaced. Engaging organizational complexity and communicating what the regulatory tax is on cybersecurity resources can help them communicate challenges, thus delivering "good" cybersecurity. The questions posed by CYBERPHOS will drive meaningful, business-driven discussions regarding cybersecurity risk and governance.

---

* Retrieved from https://en.wikipedia.org/wiki/Klingon_language

## 6.4 ACTIVE CYBERSECURITY GOVERNANCE

CYBERPHOS is Software as a Service (SaaS) with surgical consulting setup and support. Although most organizations will achieve significant improvement managing their cybersecurity risks using CYBERPHOS, we recognize some organizations will require advisory support. Situations requiring advisory support include:

- Managing a significant cybersecurity incident
- Mitigating significant cybersecurity posture deficiencies
- Developing a cybersecurity improvements blueprint
- Assessing the cybersecurity team

Unlike traditional advisory services, CYBERPHOS SaaS provides a continuous capability with advisory services only when required.

CYBERPHOS analyzes an organization's cybersecurity posture, both in absolute and relative terms. Your organization is compared to peer organizations to provide context to the indicators of cybersecurity posture and competence. Industry indicators are baked in, as different industries have different challenges and threat actors.

CYBERPHOS has both permissioned web and mobile device dashboards to enable continuous engagement of this critical risk domain.

## 6.5 CYBERPHOS HYPERLEDGER®

Hyperledger is a project created to support the development of open source blockchains and tools that enable enterprises to create distributed ledgers. It acts as a hub for different distributed ledger frameworks and libraries and offers the necessary framework, standards, guidelines, and tools to build open source blockchains and related applications for use across various industries.

Hyperledgers can be used to improve the efficiency, performance, and transactions for business processes.

CYBERPHOS has a permissioned Hyperledger to enable the permissioned sharing of cybersecurity posture information among customers. It enables the secure sharing of:

- Peer comparison metrics
- Vendor cybersecurity posture and alerts
- Regulatory reporting
- Usage metrics to drive continuous cybersecurity oversight
- Vendor tool requirements for success

Smart contracts, built into CYBERPHOS, enable the sharing of information with peers without exposing sensitive details that could be used to identify the peer organization. Smart contracts ensure that only those participants that share anonymized information will have access to peer-comparison data.

Smart contracts can also be used to monitor and measure leadership engagement for internal uses as well as a method to prove leadership engagement to stakeholders and regulators.

The CYBERPHOS Hyperledger has built-in encryption, smart contracts, permissioned ledgers, and other features to enable effective and secure data sharing in the CYBERPHOS network. There are few limits to the features we can deploy using blockchain Hyperledger.

Using CYBERPHOS tokens, the network enforces a give-to-get model for accessing peer-comparison data. The blockchain will enable this information to be normalized and anonymized in order to publish reliable and current peer-comparison information. Today, these comparisons are difficult to obtain and rarely provide normalized, current reference data to drive meaningful comparisons.

The CYBERPHOS Hyperledger enables vendors to securely share their cybersecurity posture and incidents with customers. This will increase the fidelity and reduce the cost of vendor risk analysis. It will move vendor risk from a yearly audit to continuous monitoring.

## 6.6 SUMMARY

CYBERPHOS looks at items that distract or dilute resources from the highest-priority cybersecurity efforts. We call these items taxes:

- **Complexity tax.** The greater the business, technology, and vendor complexity, the more difficult it becomes to protect critical assets.
- **Regulatory tax.** Regulators require assessments, filings, and responses to **Prove** cybersecurity. These requirements pull resources way from **Doing** cybersecurity.
- **Partner tax.** Business partners require assessments and accommodations to **Prove** cybersecurity. These requirements pull resources way from **Doing** cybersecurity.
- **Focus tax.** Incidents from peer organizations and leadership inquiries can shift attention away from an organization's cybersecurity priorities. For example, an article in the press chronicles a sophisticated attack and the cybersecurity team must respond to how they prevent such a compromise. Such a sophisticated attack vector is not relevant to an organization that has basic holes in their cybersecurity defenses.

In a perfect world, we would not need cybersecurity. Technology would work without interference, there would be no malicious actors, and users would never make mistakes. Unfortunately, the opposite is true. Technology systems are open and invite malicious exploits, bad actors are multiplying in numbers and sophistication, and users constantly make errors that allow bad things to happen. CYBERPHOS views cybersecurity as a tax on the organization—cybertax—and as with other forms of taxation, the goal is to minimize and optimize this tax.

Cybertax encompasses all resources required to provide and prove cybersecurity. This includes prevention, monitoring, remediation, improvements, and proving. Proving is an underappreciated aspect of cybertax. This includes all assessments by business partners, auditors, and regulators. In effect, it's a tax on top of the cybertax. Proving drains resources from doing, further complicating the efficient and effective deployment of cybersecurity resources.

Cybersecurity is required for all organizations, large and small. Cybertax is unavoidable. There are no cybertax-free zones. The technologies that support ubiquitous access for permissioned users and systems can be exploited by malicious actors to achieve their goals. As the Internet of Things (IoT) expands, so does the surface area for cybersecurity attacks beyond traditional computer systems. For those of you that see good cybersecurity as a positive attribute for an organization, we agree that cybersecurity is an acceptable way to differentiate your organization from your competitors. That said, managing the efficiency and effectiveness of resources applied to cybersecurity is imperative for any organization. Viewing cybersecurity through the cybertax lens provides an effective way for non–cybersecurity experts in leadership to manage and govern cybersecurity in their organizations.

An important concept in CYBERPHOS is velocity. Our dashboard tracks the velocity of:

- Complexity
- Incidents
- Maturity
- Taxation, and
- Capability

Monitoring the velocity of these items over time drives business-driven discussions with cybersecurity leadership.

CYBERPHOS drives proactive discussions regarding cybersecurity governance. Most governance discussions are reactive, driven by incidents, regulatory findings, or an article in the *Wall*

*Street Journal.* CYBERPHOS is useful for reactive discussion, but it is best used to drive thoughtful discussions regarding cybersecurity risk and the best business decisions to improve the organization's cybersecurity posture and competency.

Given the ubiquity of cybersecurity risk and the unlimited potential harm, leadership must be more engaged. This does not mean that leadership must become cybersecurity geeks. Rather, cybersecurity risk must be understood, monitored, and managed like other significant business risks, like a business tax.

Although hundreds of billions of dollars a year are spent on monitoring and preventing cybersecurity events, cybersecurity governance has not moved forward. Leadership is poorly equipped, with information that is dated and rarely correlated to business risk to properly provide cybersecurity governance. It's an obsolete island of analog information in a digital world.

CYBERPHOS delivers a continuously updated dashboard and key metrics to guide leadership's understanding of the organization's cybersecurity posture, its progress, and questions that engage both leadership and security experts in a common framework.

## 6.7 CONCLUSION

Like any well-executed business function, you must find the right balance of talent, technology, and policies. This, coupled with metrics to continuously measure the effectiveness of the cybersecurity function is imperative for success. Success in this context is preventing incidents that land you in the *Wall Street Journal* or in front of regulators. The Seven C's method was created to bring business rigor to the cybersecurity function. It's also designed to help leadership understand the impact of business decisions on cybersecurity effectiveness.

No organization can prevent all cybersecurity incidents. Operating and measuring the cybersecurity function like other key aspects of the business will yield superior results and a better understanding between business leadership and the cybersecurity function.

## REFERENCES

1. Dalio, R. (2017). *Principles: Life and Work.* New York (NY): Simon & Schuster.

# Glossary

| | |
|---|---|
| API | Application programming interface |
| APT | Advanced persistent threat |
| | |
| BoD | Board of Directors |
| | |
| CEO | Chief executive officer |
| CFO | Chief financial officer |
| CIS | Center for Internet Security |
| CISO | Chief information security officer |
| CISSP | Certified Information Systems Security Professional |
| CVEs | Common Vulnerabilities and Exposures |
| | |
| DDoS | Distributed denial-of-service |
| | |
| FTP | File transfer protocol |
| | |
| GRC | Governance, risk, and compliance |
| | |
| IA | Information assurance |
| IoA | Indicators of attack |
| IoT | Internet of Things |
| IP | Intellectual property |
| | |
| M&As | Mergers and acquisitions |
| | |
| NRT | Near real-time |

| PII | Personally identifiable information |
| PHI | Personal health information |
| PITAC | President's Information Technology Advisory Committee |

| ROI | Return on investment |

| SaaS | Software as a Service |
| SCADA | Supervisory Control and Data Acquisition |
| SDL | Security development lifecycle |
| SDLC | Software development life cycle |
| SEM | Security event management |
| SIEM | Security information and event management |
| SIM | Security information management |
| SOCs | Security operation centers |

| VPN | Virtual private network |

| WWW | World Wide Web |

# Index

(*Continued*)

## V

velocity, 8, 9, 95, 96, 107
virtual private network,
    44
vulnerability assessment,
    18, 19
vulnerability management,
    18, 19

## W

web shell, 57
World Wide Web, 35

## Z

zero day, 62
Zero Trust, 3, 6, 14

Printed in the United States
by Baker & Taylor Publisher Services